ADVANCE PRAISE

"A take-no-prisoners guide to selling digital marketing services from an industry veteran! Use it to start winning—and hope your competitors do not pick up a copy."

—TIM ASH, INTERNATIONAL MARKETING KEYNOTE SPEAKER, BEST-SELLING AUTHOR OF *UNLEASH YOUR PRIMAL BRAIN* AND *LANDING PAGE OPTIMIZATION*

"Just like his live presentations, this book delivers a ton of practical strategies anyone can use to increase leads and sales. Read, implement, and reap the rewards."

—DENNIS YU, CEO, BLITZMETRICS

"Forrest trained our team to sell conversion rate optimization services. His insights on the industry opened up new ways of seeing our business and provided a great framework we could follow. You can get the same world-class approach by reading this book. It's packed with actionable strategies that work in the real world."

—TIM DOWLING, CEO, TRUSTEDSITE

"*The blueprint Forrest lays out in this book is an essential tool for anyone who wants to differentiate their services and take revenue to the next level. It's clear that the pragmatic process he presents was battle tested in the trenches. Most importantly, it works really well.*"

—RUSSELL OWENS, PRINCIPAL, VIM VENTURES

"*Sales has never been my strong suit. I just never got it. All that changed after sitting on many sales calls with Forrest. His approach, methodologies, and tactics transformed how I viewed sales, and his battle-tested strategies helped me start closing high-value deals regularly...If it worked for me, it can 100 percent work for you. If digital sales are a mystery, you MUST buy this book.*"

—CHRIS KIDWELL, FOUNDER, CLIXO SEARCH

"*Forrest is my number one go-to guy when it comes to sales training. By applying proven methods in his book, I've increased my sales conversion rates over 100 percent!*"

—JOHN PFEIFFER, CEO, PPC FOR SMALL BIZ

"*Forrest understands how to sell digital marketing like few other visionaries. From developing sales strategies for his own businesses and countless clients, Forrest is a master at deploying the most effective sales tactics. I've witnessed him sell firsthand. He's a true sales ace, and you'd be well served by reading this book.*"

—RICK HIGHSMITH, MANAGING PARTNER, CLIXO SEARCH

"*I've seen Forrest transform and grow the sales department of several digital agencies. I can't believe he shared all of his techniques and sales secrets in this book. I wish I had a copy earlier in my career.*"

—MARK KUTOWY, VICE PRESIDENT OF BUSINESS DEVELOPMENT, SOCIALSEO

"*I implemented the concepts in this book, and our sales went up. We now have a repeatable proven sales process with a simple dashboard to monitor results. Additionally, Forrest's approach to designing presentations is pure gold, and the book includes tons of other techniques that have dramatically improved our approach to marketing and sales.*"

—DAVID MARLIN, CEO, METACOMET SYSTEMS

"*I was fortunate to have a front-row seat to watch Forrest develop the processes, techniques, and sales skills he shares in Clone the Ace. He's truly a master salesman and a great teacher. If you sell digital services, you need to read this book as soon as possible.*"

—TODD BARRS, VP OF DIGITAL, LEGALSHIELD

CLONE THE ACE

FORREST DOMBROW

CLONE
THE
ACE

A BATTLE-TESTED BLUEPRINT TO SELL
DIGITAL MARKETING SERVICES LIKE A PRO

HOUNDSTOOTH PRESS

CLONE THE ACE
A Battle-Tested Blueprint to Sell Digital
Marketing Services like a Pro

ISBN 978-1-5445-1611-0 *Hardcover*
978-1-5445-1610-3 *Paperback*
978-1-5445-1612-7 *Ebook*

To Mom for her unwavering love.

To Dad for his entrepreneurial inspiration.

To Brother for his never-ending support.

To Son for his joyful spirit.

Without you, there would be no ace to clone.

CONTENTS

INTRODUCTION

MY JOURNEY FROM
CLUELESS TO CLOSER

"If you want to be successful, find someone who has achieved the results you want and copy what they do, and you'll achieve the same results."

—TONY ROBBINS

As soon as he said it, I wanted to punch my boss in the face. He was standing in his office talking to the new hotshot salesperson he'd hired and didn't think I could hear him. My new coworker asked if I was any good at sales. The boss mimicked a person choking and said, "He's terrible." I was pissed.

I didn't punch him in the face—mostly because he was twice my size but also because he was right. I *was* terrible at sales. I lacked confidence and often said cringeworthy things during sales calls. Although I was a strategic marketing manager and had no desire to be a salesperson, his comment hurt.

Four years later, I faced a more difficult situation. A few coworkers and I left that digital marketing agency to start our own. A year after that, with only a handful of small clients, we parted ways with the founder in charge of sales. The two remaining partners and I were digital marketers, not salespeople. We had no marketing budget, and none of us wanted to do sales.

If we could not get new clients quickly, we would have to get nine-to-five jobs. The idea of having a "regular job" made me nauseous. I said, "Give me $50 a month for marketing, and I'll try to drum up some business." Although my partners were willing to help, from a marketing and sales perspective, it was up to me to make the agency fly or die.

Stay tuned for the exciting conclusion.

WHAT THIS BOOK WILL DO FOR YOU

When I speak with agency owners and sales managers, I hear six common complaints:

1. We're not generating enough quality leads.
2. We're having trouble closing enough good deals.
3. I'm the owner; I'm handling sales and I'm overwhelmed.
4. Every salesperson we've hired sucks.
5. We're struggling to train and scale our sales team.
6. We're having trouble retaining clients.

Whether you're an anxious agency owner, a frustrated freelancer, or a struggling sales manager, this book can help you.

You will get a battle-tested blueprint to attract more leads, sell digital marketing services like a pro, and build a scalable sales system. This book contains detailed information on the processes, techniques, templates, and skills I've refined over the course of seventeen years. I hold nothing back. You'll be able to clone my approach and produce the same record-smashing results my clients and I have enjoyed.

The sales system you'll learn is built on six core principles.

POSITION YOUR AGENCY TO WIN

Make marketing, sales, and client retention easier by positioning your agency as the best choice.

ATTRACT THE LEADS YOU NEED

Develop a marketing plan that attracts high-quality leads without pestering prospects with cold calls or spammy emails.

TAKE A TEAM SELLING APPROACH

Build a distributed sales process that produces better results without having to hire hard-to-find and expensive sales unicorns.

BE A STRATEGIC SALES DOCTOR

Transition from being an order taker to being a strategic consultant who diagnoses prospects' marketing problems and prescribes solutions that increase client retention.

CLOSE DEALS WITH AUTHENTIC, VALUE-BASED SELLING

Develop sales skills that win deals by being authentic and demonstrating the ability to help prospects achieve their bottom-line goals.

TRACK AND AUTOMATE YOUR AGENCY'S REVENUE GROWTH

Use tracking and automation to improve efficiency and effectiveness throughout your sales process.

HOW I LEARNED TO SELL AND TEACH OTHERS

After raising my hand to try sales at my fledgling agency, I reached a crossroads: get clients or get a job.

I had a $50-a-month marketing budget, no experience selling digital marketing services, and I HATED networking. I preferred to sit quietly at my computer and crank out work for clients. Small talk drained me. I used to stand in the corner at networking events stuffing my face with hors d'oeuvres to avoid talking to people.

Since the idea of getting a regular job seemed worse than doing sales, I grabbed a stack of business cards and pounded the pavement. In just a few years, we grew the agency to over a million in revenue. In chapter 4, I'll show you the exact $50-a-month marketing plan I used.

I started by reading sales books and running around town learning by trial and error. My efforts earned me an invitation to a national speaking tour, which generated lucrative referral partnerships and many high-paying clients. Because audience members voted me one of the best speakers, I was named one of the Top 40 Digital Marketing Strategists in the United States by the Online Marketing Institute.

I've spoken with nearly three thousand marketing managers and business owners looking to purchase digital marketing and have sold over $15,000,000 worth of services. I have closed deals with companies ranging from small family businesses to some of the most famous brands in the world. I know exactly what digital marketing buyers want and how to get them to pick your agency.

In 2014, I started a consulting business called Solve Sales (www.solvesales.com). I've worked with a variety of digital marketing agencies, web development shops, and freelancers to improve their branding, marketing, sales processes, and skills. Through my coaching and consulting work, I have refined my original system and taught others to get the same results I've achieved.

THE EXCITING CONCLUSION

In 2018, I had my drop-the-mic moment. I was invited to sit on an expert panel discussing sales strategies for digital agency owners. I had not seen the boss I wanted to punch in the face for about ten years. Ironically, they sat him at my table.

Earlier that day, I had been trying to close a deal with Amazon. After the panel session, I checked my phone and saw that Amazon had signed the agreement. As I sat back down at my table, I let out a "YES!" under my breath. The person sitting next to me asked what I was so excited about. I said, "I just closed an SEO deal with Amazon." The look on my old boss's face was priceless. The cringeworthy kid who was terrible at sales had turned into a sales ace.

My journey from clueless to closer has resulted in a battle-tested sales system you can use to improve sales and crush your competition. As the Tony Robbins quote at the beginning of this introduction says, you can clone me and achieve results like mine. It's a shortcut to sales success. That said, this book is not for everyone.

Clone the Ace offers an evolved, authentic approach to selling. You will not learn cheesy closing tricks that leave prospects feeling like they need a shower. I don't teach scammy sales funnels, get-rich-quick schemes, or webinar marketing hacks. This book covers a professional approach to strategic selling, tailored specifically for digital agencies and freelancers.

Even though any reader can pick up valuable sales tactics, the approach I teach will not work well for agencies that are comfortable selling snake oil to unsophisticated clients. If you're committed to excellence, want to sell services at the higher end of the fee scale, and are willing to put in the effort, the information in this book will increase your sales. Also, if you copy my system, you will be able to hire average salespeople and still produce great results.

Before we get to chugging coffee and closing clients, we need to lay the foundation for sales success. Part one of this book will help you position your agency to win more deals.

Part two will teach you the specific steps you can take to attract more leads, build a highly effective sales machine, and improve your sales skills.

LAY THE FOUNDATION FOR SALES SUCCESS

CHAPTER 1

THE SOLUTION TO ALL YOUR SALES PROBLEMS

"Eighty-five percent of the reasons for failure are deficiencies in the systems and process rather than the employee. The role of management is to change the process rather than badgering individuals to do better."

—W. EDWARDS DEMING

If you've heard the following story, bear with me. There is a critical part most people miss.

In 1954, a struggling salesman of milkshake mixers noticed that one customer was buying an unusually large number of mixers. Curious, the salesman drove to the establishment and found a super popular walk-up restaurant offering lightning-fast service at half the price of its competitors. The salesman approached the owners to find out what was behind their smashing success.

The salesman was Ray Kroc, and the restaurant was McDonald's.

As the story goes, Richard and Maurice McDonald wanted to make food more quickly and sell it for less money. The brothers temporarily closed their restaurant and designed a new system for food preparation. They called it the Speedee Service System.

Most times this story is told, the main lessons are that having an efficient, repeatable system is what allowed McDonald's to scale and that you need such a system to scale your agency. That's old, yet still important, news. It's such common knowledge that most agencies I work with have at least some documented processes for delivering their marketing services.

Although an agency may have a thirty-seven-point checklist for running Facebook ad campaigns, when it comes to their own marketing and sales, all they have is an average website, a business card, and a basic proposal. There are two main reasons that systems thinking tends to go out the window when it comes to sales:

1. Many agency owners are not salespeople. They tend to start their careers, like I did, as digital marketing practitioners (or web developers/designers). Typically, they have had no formal sales training and don't know how to build an effective sales system or team.
2. The agency owner hires an experienced salesperson and assumes they will know what to do. Later, the owner realizes that the sales "pro" can close a few deals if spoon-fed hot leads, but they are not

truly self-sufficient and don't have a repeatable sales system on which the owner can build a successful agency.

You get the point. You need an efficient, repeatable system that other people can run. That's the well-known lesson. Here's the part that's often overlooked.

THE AVERAGE ACE

When McDonald's created their Speedee Service System, there were other restaurants that made food quickly. Those restaurants used short-order cooks. Because short-order cooks had to be good at many different tasks across a wide range of menu items, they required a lot of training, skill, and practice. As a result, good short-order cooks were in short supply.

The Speedee Service System was designed like an auto assembly line. Instead of having one cook do everything, the system allowed unskilled workers to perform one specialized step in the overall food preparation process, like making the fries. It's easier to hire people to be great at one or two tasks than sixteen.

Here is a description of SOME of the tasks and skills needed to run a basic sales system:

- Develop, implement, and manage marketing campaigns that generate leads.
- Respond to, qualify, and score leads.
- Run diagnosis meetings that require knowledge about each service you offer.

- Conduct tactical research and develop strategic solutions to prospects' marketing problems.
- Create and deliver professional sales presentations that convince prospects to hire your agency.
- Customize contracts and negotiate final fees and legal terms.
- Manage a sales pipeline, close deals, and lead the onboarding process.
- Handle the administrative tasks required to support the entire sales process.

That's not even the entire list. If your current approach is to hire people who can do every marketing and sales task, change the job title from Account Executive to Sales Unicorn.

Sales unicorns do exist. However, they are rare and tend to be expensive. Even if you find a unicorn and have enough money to hire them, having them do everything on their own dramatically limits the number of deals they can close.

However, if you build a system that is repeatable AND has specialized roles, you can have two to three average people running it and still crank out great results. I encourage you to take a team selling approach, which I cover in detail throughout this book.

If you're a freelancer or a small agency that can't have three or four people running your marketing and sales, don't worry. I'll address customizing the system for your situation in chapter 12. For now, I suggest you think about lead generation, selling, and administrative work as three separate roles.

SURPRISE! YOU ALREADY HAVE A SALES SYSTEM

"Each system is perfectly designed to give you exactly what you are getting today."

—W. EDWARDS DEMING

After reading the McDonald's story, you may have had one of the following thoughts:

- Yeah, totally makes sense. I don't have a sales system and I obviously need one.
- Well, I kind of have a system, but it's not producing the results I want.
- We're small and have modest growth goals. Do I really need a fancy system?

If your agency is up and running, you have a system. You may not have created it consciously. It may be missing critical parts. You may run it inconsistently. But make no mistake, you have a way that you typically generate and respond to leads and present your services. As the Deming quote points out, the results you're getting from your system are due to how it's designed and run, not because you don't have a system.

In his book *Atomic Habits*, James Clear suggests that if you're not hitting your goals, your goals are not the problem—your system is. Goals are the results you want to produce. Systems and processes are what you do to produce them. Changing your goals is not going to change your results. Changing your systems and processes can.

So you have a system. What you need is a COMPLETE

system that has been PROVEN to produce the results you want, WITHOUT unicorns running it.

WHAT A COMPLETE SYSTEM INCLUDES

"If you can't describe what you are doing as a process, you don't know what you're doing."

— W. EDWARDS DEMING

Let's define a few terms so you are clear about what a complete system includes.

SYSTEM

A system is a collection of components organized to produce a particular outcome. Mass transit is a good example. Its purpose is to move people from one location to another as efficiently as possible. Each McDonald's restaurant is a system, designed to deliver crappy food quickly. Your system is what you do, in what order, to produce leads and sales.

PROCESS

A process is a series of step-by-step actions taken to achieve *part* of the overall outcome. How a bus driver collects your fare is a process. The steps each McDonald's employee takes to make a Big Mac is a process. Your sales processes are how to do what your system tells you to do.

TEMPLATE

A template is a document or file with a preset format. An

electronic form you fill out to buy a bus pass is a template. The buns and burgers at McDonald's are physical templates that help employees assemble each burger the right way. Templates are what you use to execute your processes correctly and efficiently.

TOOL

Tools allow you to build and run a system. The card you use to store and spend your bus fare is a tool. The bus is itself a tool. The specialized fryers and cooking machines at McDonald's are tools. In sales systems, tools include things like email platforms, customer relationship management (CRM) platforms, and web conferencing software.

SKILL

Although the right system can eliminate the need to hire unicorns, the people running your system still need some level of skill, motivation, and attention to detail. Someone has to drive the bus and set the french fry machine to the right temperature. Skills are not part of a system, but they are necessary to run and maintain a healthy one. After all, we're selling five-, six-, and seven-figure marketing programs, not $1 burgers.

DOCUMENTATION

To be consistent and scalable, your system should not live in your head. Even if you work by yourself, it's a good idea to spend a little time getting everything down on digital paper. Documenting your system helps internalize it and provides a resource you can use if you need to train people in the future. Also, documented processes can increase the value of your agency should you want to sell it down the road. Consider creating a system overview document to let people know "how it's done here."

Your overview document should contain all your system steps, define terms, and highlight your general methodology for selling. Also, it should list and describe the processes used for each step.

Create checklists as necessary and link to each template so new sales reps learning your system can quickly access the documents they'll need to run each process.

HOW THIS BOOK IS STRUCTURED

The rest of part one will help you lay the foundation for sales success. Part two covers the details of building and running a successful sales system. Each chapter covers one step in the system and has the following basic format:

- An overview of the step
- The processes for completing the step
- The skills you need to execute each process successfully

Chapter 11 shows you how to track your results and improve efficiency by using tools, templates, and automation. Chapter 12 provides ways to customize the system for your specific needs. There are plenty of examples throughout, and at the end, I provide a link to additional templates and resources you can download.

Now that you know the importance of having the right

kind of system, the next chapter will cover a critical concept you need to nail before you start building your sales machine.

KEY TAKEAWAYS FROM CHAPTER 1

- To scale your sales function, you need a repeatable system.

- To avoid the need to hire expensive sales unicorns, you need to break down your system into specialized steps and take a team selling approach.

- You have a sales system. If it's not producing the results you want, it's not that you don't have a system; it's that something is missing or not being executed properly.

- You don't necessarily need to change your goals or people. You need to create a complete system that consistently produces the results you want.

- A complete, documented system includes processes, templates, tools, and the basic sales skills necessary to run it effectively.

CHAPTER 2

POSITION YOUR AGENCY TO WIN

"Good jockeys will do well on good horses but not on broken-down nags."

—WARREN BUFFETT

In Formula One racing, the car that posts the fastest qualifying lap gets the pole position. The pole is the inside starting position on the front row of cars. From the beginning of Formula One racing in 1950 through the Korean Grand Prix in 2012, drivers starting in the pole position have won more than 40 percent of the races.[1]

From 2014 through the end of the 2018 race season, team Mercedes dominated the sport, winning 74 percent of all the races. During the 2016 season, Mercedes grabbed every pole position, and their pole to win rate was 87 percent, more than double the historical rate of 40 percent.

---

[1]   "Pole Position," Fandom.com, accessed December 30, 2020, https://f1.fandom.com/wiki/Pole_Position#cite_note-0.

In 2019, Mercedes started the season by winning the first eight races. Mercedes was so good that before the races started, most people assumed that unless both of their cars hit the wall and burst into flames, the other teams had practically no chance to win.

What's the source of their insane success?

In 2014, Formula One racing made one of the biggest rule changes in the history of the sport. Race teams had to switch from naturally aspirated 2.4 liter V8 engines to turbocharged 1.6-liter V6s. I don't know what that means, so don't worry if you're not a car nut.

Mercedes engineers made one simple change to the turbocharger used in the new engines. Their team split the turbo in half and arranged the parts to make the engine produce fifty more horsepower than the standard configuration used by the other teams.

Although many race teams employ champion-level drivers, Mercedes dominates mainly because their cars are faster than everyone else's. They don't have better jockeys; they have better horses.

Whether you're in a car race or a horse race, starting in front of everyone else is a big advantage. However, as Mr. Buffett's quote points out, if you put a great driver in a slow car (or on a slow horse), they'll never win the pole position, let alone the main race.

Some estimates put the total number of digital marketing and traditional advertising agencies in the United States at 120,000.[2] Many sales situations pit you against at least two to three other agencies or freelancers. Selling digital marketing services can be like a competitive car race.

If you use the positioning techniques I'm about to share with you to create a unique advantage, like Mercedes did, you can start sales races at the front of the pack and win deals more easily, even if you don't have an ace salesperson at the wheel.

All you have to do is make a small tweak to your agency's engine.

EASY MONEY: HOW TO BUILD A FAST CAR AND POSITION IT IN FRONT OF THE PACK

The continuum below shows three different kinds of products/services.

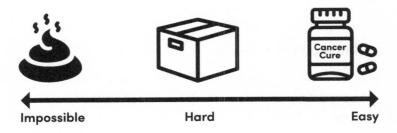

Impossible   **Hard**   **Easy**

On the left side is a lump of poop. This extreme example represents a product or service that is so inferior to other options that nobody would purchase it, for any price, from any salesperson.

2   Brian Regienczuk, "Let's Reinvent How Businesses and Creative Agencies Connect," AgencySpotter.com, accessed December 30, 2020, https://co.agencyspotter.com/lets-reinvent-how-businesses-find-agencies-and-work-together/.

In the middle is a generic brown box that represents products or services that are good but look pretty much like the other options. This is what most agencies offer: generic services that they present in similar ways to their competitors. They start the sales race in the middle of the pack, with an average engine.

Now imagine creating a cure for cancer with minimal side effects. You'd have no competition. You could be the most incompetent salesperson in the world with no website, no sales system, or even an email address and you'd still sell a zillion pills. Easy money.

To have a marketing and sales advantage over your competitors, you don't have to create a miracle pill. You just have to split the turbo and crank out a measly fifty more horsepower. Offer something a little bit unique and shift your agency to the right of the generic brown boxes. Let me show you how.

BEING THE BEST CHOICE

All buyers try to determine "the best choice." When you go car shopping, you're looking for the best vehicle for your budget. When buying a home, you want the best house. Even when shopping for a $10 T-shirt, you're going to spend a few minutes comparing your options so you can pick the best shirt for your needs.

Digital marketing buyers do the same thing. Although prospects may consider a variety of different factors (price, years of experience, etc.), they all have one question at the core of their decision-making process:

Which agency do I believe is most likely to produce the results I want, at a price I can afford?

The prospect is not thinking about which agency can do the best paid search (or whatever service they are considering). They are asking themselves which agency they *BELIEVE* can *PRODUCE* the best *RESULTS*. During the early part of the sales process, it's all about perception. Also, the prospect is looking for someone to use digital marketing tactics to produce bottom-line results, not to simply complete the tasks listed in the service agreement.

If a prospect cannot identify at least one reason you appear to offer the best chance to hit their business goals, more often than not, you will lose the deal. One of my favorite business books of all time, *Blue Ocean Strategy*, frames your positioning task perfectly when it encourages readers to "make the competition irrelevant."

You can't be the best choice for every type of prospect. As such, the first step in positioning yourself to win is to answer the following question:

For which type of clients can I be the best choice?

PLAY WINNABLE GAMES: YOUR IDEAL CLIENT PROFILE

Many years ago, the CEO of a successful digital development agency told me a story that stuck in my memory. He'd come across a case study about a hospital that had a 95 percent success rate on a particular medical procedure. I don't recall the industry average, but this hospital's 95 percent success rate was WAY higher than that of other medical facilities that performed the same procedure.

The hospital's success rate was so high because they identified several factors that indicated when the procedure would be successful and when it would not. Once they set the criteria, they were ultrastrict about which patients qualified to work with their doctors. If a particular person did not meet the success criteria, they would not perform the procedure.

The hospital positioned themselves to succeed because they created what I call a Winnable Game. A Winnable Game is a scenario that indicates you have a high likelihood of success. You have a good chance not only of winning the sale but of delivering great results, too. Once the hospital established their extremely high success rate, it became a powerful marketing and sales tool that attracted even more patients. The hospital created the perception that they were clearly the best choice for the procedure—which they were, for specific people in specific situations.

ACE IN THE HOLE

Play Winnable Games. Identify characteristics of clients for whom you're certain your services will produce excellent results, and you'll vastly increase client satisfaction, client retention, and profitability. Also, by adhering strictly to your stated criteria, you start a virtuous cycle that leads to increased referrals, more new clients, and happy employees.

As I mentioned at the end of the last section, you can't be the best option for everyone. Even though Mercedes has the best Formula One car, they would barely get off the starting line in a motocross race on a dirt track. Their engines and cars are designed to do well in a very specific type of race, to the exclusion of just about every other type.

To make it easier to attract leads, win deals, and retain clients, you have to work only with clients you are confident you can make happy. Having a clear picture of your ideal client will help you find Winnable Games.

As you work through the next few sections, keep in mind that in order for unique positioning to work, it has to be relevant to your prospect. Saying you specialize in lead generation for plumbers may be unique, but it's totally irrelevant to e-commerce companies. You can't make your positioning relevant if you don't know exactly whom you're targeting. To begin creating your ideal client profile(s), ask yourself the following question:

> What factors or circumstances indicate our services can truly help someone such that they represent a Winnable Game for our agency?

- Is it their industry?
- Is it a specific internet marketing problem you're good at solving?
- Is it a certain budget level or specific service need that matches your team's skills?
- Which factors are absolute requirements versus those that are "nice to have"?
- Are there any red flags that indicate a bad fit?

When I started writing this book, I considered positioning it for a broader audience. Can the information in this book help a software company or a financial consultant sell more services? Sure. However, because the majority of my experience and case studies are specific to digital marketing agencies, they are my ideal clients. I focused the title and content of the book on the type of prospects to whom my book and my consulting services have the greatest chance of looking like the best choice.

Take the time to sketch out your ideal client profile and keep it front and center as you begin to position your agency. Ask your employees, especially the ones who work with clients day in and day out, for input. Here are a few questions you can ask your team:

- What kinds of clients do you like working with best?
- Which of our current clients do you love the most? Why?
- In what situations do we do our best work and produce the best results?
- Where are we already seeing strong demand and solid results?
- What are the five to ten factors that indicate we have a Winnable Game on your hands?

Below is a sample format you can use. If you do a Google search for "ideal client profile template," you'll get plenty of other examples. Customize it to your needs. You can create profiles for each service you offer. If you have two or three ideal client types, make a profile for each. It's rarely a good idea to have more than three, as you can start to lose focus and your positioning can become watered down.

Company Profile	
Industry	Accounting and financial services
Size	At least 25 people and/or $5,000,000 in annual revenue
Their Target Market	B2B services for mid-size companies
Their Geographic Focus	US only
Budget	Monthly marketing budget of at least $10,000
Internal Resources	3 members on their marketing team and in-house designers
Prospect Profile	
Job Title	Director of Marketing
Pain Points	They need an agency that can be more responsive, proactive, and responsible for helping them hit their lead generation goals.
Personality Traits	An engaged professional with reasonable expectations
Key Needs/Wants	They need better results from their paid search campaigns on Google Ads. When I look at their current campaigns, there are glaring mistakes and areas for improvement.
Marketing Experience	Experienced in general, but not super savvy about the nitty-gritty of paid search

ACE IN THE HOLE

Remember that this is your ideal client profile. Most prospects will not perfectly fit every criterion. Use it as a guide. Be clear on which factors are essential and which are nice to have. Depending on your goals and current financial needs, you may choose to use your customer profiles very strictly, like the hospital with a 95 percent success rate, or a bit more loosely.

HOW TO FIND THE BEST FISHING HOLE

Before we get to the second fundamental positioning

decision, I want to share something I created called the Fishing Framework. The Fishing Framework will help you make sure your ideal client profile(s) are viable and set you up for successful lead attraction.

Gary Halbert was one of the most famous and successful direct response copywriters in history. He wrote a series of letters to his clients to teach them his methods. Here is a snippet from one of my favorite letters:

> "If you and I both owned a hamburger stand and we were in a contest to see who could sell the most hamburgers, what advantages would you most like to have on your side to help you win?"

> The answers vary. Some of the students say they would like to have the advantage of having superior meat from which to make their burgers. Others say they want sesame seed buns. Others mention location. Someone usually wants to be able to offer the lowest prices.

> And so on.

> Whatever. In any case, after my students are finished telling me what advantages they would most like to have, I usually say to them something like this: "O.K., I'll give you every single advantage you have asked for. I, myself, only want one advantage and, if you will give it to me, I will (when it comes to selling burgers) whip the pants off all of you!"

> "What advantage do you want?" they ask.

> "The only advantage I want," I reply...

"Is...A Starving Crowd!"

Think about it. When it comes to direct marketing, the most profitable habit you can cultivate is the habit of constantly being on the lookout for groups of people (markets) who have demonstrated that they are starving (or, at least hungry) for some particular product or service.[3]

The hungrier your target prospects, the easier it is to attract them and the less sales skills you need to win them over. With the starving crowd concept in mind, let's review the Fishing Framework.

The Empty Pond

The Empty Pond has either no or very few fish in it. You can find yourself in an empty pond if you go too narrow with your ideal client profile or pick a dying industry.

For example, if you focus on law firms, that's good. But if you focus only on law firms that specialize in maritime law in Minnesota, that's a pond with very few, if any, fish in it.

The Crowded Pond

The Crowded Pond has lots of fish but also lots of other fishermen. You can find yourself in a crowded pond when you go too broad with your ideal client profile.

For example, if you focus on designing websites for small businesses, you'll find a ton of hungry fish, but also lots of competitors offering low-cost or free site-building tools.

---

3   "The Gary Halbert Letter," TheGaryHalbertLetter.com, accessed December 30, 2020, http://www.thegaryhalbertletter.com/.

The Satisfied Pond

Regardless of the number of fish or competitors, the Satisfied Pond is a poor choice because the fish are not hungry for what you offer.

For example, if you focus on people who own franchise restaurants, national franchise fees may include internet marketing and thus the individual franchisees have no appetite for your services. Wealth managers who cater to the super rich and tend to get their clients from country club referrals, rather than Google search, are another example.

The Profitable Pond

As Goldilocks would say, the Profitable Pond is just right. It's got enough hungry fish and limited competition. Examples include the following:

1. Paid search specialists for women's clothing brands
2. Web design and digital marketing for hotels and resorts
3. Amazon Marketplace consulting for manufacturers trying to sell directly to consumers

---

The title of this section is a bit of a misnomer. Although you may want to conduct some research, your task is not so much to *find* the best fishing hole as it is to *create* it through your positioning decisions.

The Profitable Pond examples listed above illustrate the point. Web design focused on the hospitality industry is not a pond that exists anywhere until you create it by declaring it as your focus. It's like making up the rules of your own Winnable Game. With a bit of creativity, you can even transform a Crowded Pond (websites for small businesses) into a Profitable Pond (websites for plastic surgery practices).

If you do it right, you're likely to be one of the only agencies fishing in your particular pond. On the other hand, if you don't pick a pond consciously, you'll be drifting in the big sea of competition with no real marketing or sales advantages.

There are a lot of digital marketing agencies and freelancers. Many struggle with sales and are hungry for help. There are very few, if any, sales consultants who specialize in helping digital marketing agencies increase leads and sales. I created a Winnable Game in a Profitable Pond. As a result, everything about marketing, sales, and producing good results for my clients is easier.

Once you have nailed down your ideal client profile, you can move on to the second step in the positioning process.

WHAT KIND OF AGENCY DO YOU WANT TO BE WHEN YOU GROW UP?

There are five different types of agencies, and you want to match your agency type to your ideal client profile. For example, a large fancy agency that works with companies like Coca-Cola and Nike is not going to be a fit for a local yoga studio.

The type of agency you decide to be and how well it matches your ideal client profile will have a big impact on your marketing strategy, your pricing strategy, and your sales success.

In no particular order, here are the five types of agencies.

FREELANCER OR SMALL GROUP

This is a solopreneur or group of two to five people offering one specific service (such as article writing for blogs) or acting as a jack-of-all-trades offering "digital marketing" more broadly. Whether specialist or generalist, such an agency may offer low-end, cookie-cutter services for small clients or higher-priced, expert-level programs for more-sophisticated companies.

BIG-BOX AGENCY

These are your large agencies with hundreds of employees. Big-box agencies tend to offer cookie-cutter marketing services for small businesses. The scope of work, price, and delivery process are usually exactly the same for every client. These agencies are the Walmarts of the industry. Their calling card is low-cost, generic services.

Examples of big-box agencies are Yellow Pages (YP.com) or Yelp, which tend to offer low-cost advertising programs for small businesses.

SMALL-TO-MIDSIZE BASIC

These agencies typically have five to fifty employees and offer basic, inexpensive services for small companies. For example, they may offer websites for $2,500 or basic social media packages for $750 a month. Their services may be a bit more sophisticated and flexible than those of the big-box agencies but not by much. They're like Old Navy, inexpensive but functional for the right kind of customer.

SMALL-TO-MIDSIZE BOUTIQUE

Although each agency type has its place, the boutique agency model is the one I've worked with the most and like the best.

These agencies are similar in size to the basic agency but offer higher-priced, expert-level services. They tend to target clients in what I call the fat middle.

The fat middle consists of companies that are doing a million to a few hundred million in yearly sales and have some in-house marketing resources but need to outsource specific tasks. They expect to pay around $2,500 to $10,000 a month for each marketing service. If engaged in paid online advertising, they spend anywhere from $10,000 to $250,000 a month on their media budget.

Although they can provide good value, these agencies are like local, higher-end clothing boutiques—great stuff at fair prices but not cheap.

MADISON AVENUE

These are your huge, global agencies like McKinsey or Ogilvy. They work with large clients under seven-figure engagements, employ top-level experts, and can staff large teams to execute sophisticated, multichannel campaigns. Madison Avenue agencies can be overpriced compared to boutiques with top-level talent, as clients may pay a premium for the agency's famous name and expensive offices. These agencies are like the Nordstroms of the industry— big, fancy, and pricey.

Your agency already fits into one of these buckets—if not exactly, then at least closely enough. Did you choose a bucket consciously, or did you just fall into it? Does your agency type match your ideal client profile and skills?

REFINE YOUR POSITIONING THROUGH YOUR SERVICE STRATEGY

The specific mix of services you offer, the way you deliver them, and the way you price them are all powerful ways to position your agency as the best choice. The agency descriptions I covered in the last section point to the kinds of services each type might offer. However, two agencies of the same type can have different service mixes and pricing strategies.

COOKIE-CUTTER PROGRAMS

Cookie-cutter programs are static, fixed engagements. They are exactly the same for every customer, and they generally don't change much, if at all, over the life of the client relationship. Cookie-cutter services tend to be low cost (say, $99—$1,500 a month) and are often offered in levels such as bronze, silver, and gold.

Cookie-cutter services are easy to describe on a sales call. Showing a tidy chart with check marks indicating what's included at each level helps less-sophisticated buyers understand their options. Many prospects (and order-taker salespeople) love the simple, set-package sort of presentation.

Cookie-cutter programs can be good for the efficiency, profitability, and scalability of your agency, too. When you deliver essentially the same work over and over, you can create easy-to-follow checklists and hire less-experienced marketers to run your processes.

On the other hand, cookie-cutter programs have several drawbacks. People don't buy digital marketing services because they want digital marketing. What they actually want is to generate more leads or sales, and many cookie-cutter programs fail to produce the results clients want.

For example, a $199-per-month link-building program is not SEO. It's a small part of SEO. If the client is SEO-savvy and just needs to outsource the link-building portion of their larger SEO strategy, fine. However, most small business owners don't have a larger SEO strategy and don't really understand that a $199 link-building program is not likely to produce more sales by itself. It's like hiring a plumber and expecting them to build an entire house. Cookie-cutter programs often lead to unwinnable games and cause expensive client churn.

ACE IN THE HOLE

Nobody wants digital marketing services. They want the results those services can produce: namely, increased leads and sales. Whatever type of services you offer, make sure they are designed to produce the bottom-line results your target clients crave. Producing profitable results is the only way to retain clients over the long term.

Although I personally do not advocate for cookie-cutter programs, I acknowledge that some agencies are very successful selling them, and in some situations, they can be an appropriate choice for customers. If cookie-cutter programs work for you and your ideal clients, don't let me stop you. To retain clients and be able to sleep at night, just make sure that what you offer can produce results that will satisfy your clients. Happy clients are one of the cornerstones of a profitable agency.

TACTICAL SPECIALISTS

Tactical specialists offer one to three highly specialized services, each delivered at or near expert level. To better match specific client needs and produce results, services tend to be flexible and complement each other.

For example, I worked with an agency that offered world-class SEO, paid search, and conversion optimization. Although they did have some static packages with fixed prices, most of their programs could be customized. If an SEO client was having technical issues, the agency would focus more heavily on that area. If the client needed lots of content creation, their budget could be used for that. Rather than having a static scope of work, the agency would adjust their focus over time to meet real-world priorities, while always staying within the specific tactic they were hired to handle.

Tactical specialists typically work with midsize clients and charge $2,500–$10,000 per service.

FULL-SERVICE FLEXIBLE

In the full-service flexible approach, the agency might offer branding, logo design, digital strategy, website development, and ongoing management of a variety of digital marketing campaigns. This service strategy is like offering an outsourced or fractional marketing department that can deliver a variety of digital marketing services for one monthly fee.

For example, rather than charging a client $5,000 a month for content marketing, they can charge the client

$7,500 a month for "digital marketing." Then each month, the agency and the client decide the priorities, and the agency shifts its work among a broad set of services and tactics. During some periods, they may be heavily focused on paid advertising and landing pages and at other times on something completely different such as influencer campaigns.

FIXED-FEE PROJECTS

Some people love offering projects because you get a bunch of money at once and don't have prickly relationships that drag on over time. Other people dislike projects because cash flow is less predictable and the costs to ramp teams up and down puts a dent in profitability. Regardless of your opinion on projects, certain types of work (such as building a microsite or conducting a one-time social media audit) are well suited to be sold as a fixed-fee project.

For many agencies, offering monthly retainer-based services along with fixed-fee projects allows them to address a variety of sales scenarios.

Regardless of which service strategy you take, you have options within the strategy. Here are a few examples of other ways you can slice and dice the services you offer:

- Flat fees versus hourly fees versus a percentage of media spend (for online advertising)
- Short-term pilot programs that prove the viability of a tactic
- Pay for performance, where you are paid for specific results, such as by the lead or sale

- Audits that provide recommendations clients can implement on their own
- Training along the way so a client can become self-sufficient
- Month-to-month versus six-month or twelve-month contracts

The key is to select the service and pricing approach that best matches the needs of your target customers and positions your agency as clearly the best choice.

THREE SHORTCUTS TO WIN THE POLE POSITION

If you've done the work I've covered thus far in this chapter, you should already be somewhat well positioned for at least one ideal client type. This section contains additional detail and specific steps you can take to truly nail your positioning.

SHORTCUT #1: BE A SPECIALIST

"You cannot be everything to everyone. If you decide to go north, you cannot go south at the same time."

—JEROEN DE FLANDER

There is a business axiom I hear all the time that says, "The riches are in the niches." Specializing in a specific niche is the quickest and easiest way to differentiate yourself. Also, specialization provides numerous marketing, sales, and operational advantages. Although I've touched on specialization a few times in this chapter, I want to look at this shortcut in a bit more detail because it's just that powerful. Here's an example.

If you hurt your knee skiing and needed surgery, which of these doctors would you pick?

Doctor A	Doctor B
• 10 years of experience • Orthopedic surgeon • Over 100 successful surgeries	• 10 years of experience • Orthopedic surgeon who specializes in knee injuries from skiing • Over 100 successful knee surgeries on patients injured while skiing

All else being equal, Doctor B has won before the race has even started. Buyers of agency services go through the same thought process. When you specialize in solving the exact problem your prospect faces, your specialization implies that you're better and more efficient than a generalist. Note also that if you hurt your wrist playing Frisbee, Doctor B would lose. As I said earlier, your area of specialization must be relevant to your ideal audience, and you can't be the best choice for everyone.

One of my clients focused its agency services exclusively on e-commerce websites. Because of that specialization, before I even opened my mouth to do any "selling," prospects would frequently say things like, "I love that you focus on e-commerce. None of the other agencies I'm considering have that specific expertise, and I think you guys might be the best option for us." That agency was often in the pole position just from making the decision to specialize.

Here are eight ways you can specialize. Feel free to pick one or combine several for a truly unique fishing pond. Just don't go too narrow and end up in an empty one.

1. By industry: accounting, clothing, restaurants, software, etc.
2. By company type: small, large, B2B, B2C, private, public, or nonprofits
3. By website type: e-commerce, lead generation, informational, or entertainment
4. By service type: full service, one service or platform specific (e.g., Facebook advertising experts)
5. By price point: are you the Fiat, Honda, Lexus, or Ferrari of your industry?
6. By fee structure: flat fee, monthly retainer, pay per performance, or hourly
7. By business model: services delivered by consultants versus automated tools versus selling leads you generate through your own web properties
8. By geographic region: select a city, state, or region you can blanket with marketing to become the dominant player in that area

SHORTCUT #2: OFFER A UNIQUE SERVICE MIX

When I started as a Strategic Marketing Manager back in 2004, the only thing most businesses cared about was building a five-page brochure website and getting ranked number one on Google. Very few people had even heard of paid search advertising or Facebook.

Since I was new to internet marketing, the owner of the agency (the one I wanted to punch in the face) asked me to sit down with each employee and learn what they did for our clients.

As I was getting up to speed, I spotted a book in the office titled *Persuasive Online Copywriting, with an Afterword on Conversion Rate Optimization.* If at the time hardly anyone knew what pay-per-click advertising was, basically nobody in the world, except the authors of the book and a handful of other people, knew about conversion rate optimization. If you're not familiar with the term, it's the art and science of improving a website's user experience and content so that more visitors buy something or convert to a lead.

While reading the book and meeting all the people at the agency, a question hit me like a bolt of lightning. I thought, "Okay, she's making logos and pretty websites. That guy is running the paid search ads to drive traffic. That team is doing the SEO stuff. And that woman is managing the projects. Who is making sure these clients actually convert all the website traffic into leads and sales?"

The answer: nobody.

At the time, nobody I ran into at the agency (or in the industry) was talking about conversion rate optimization. I thought this was insane. If not to generate leads and sales, what was the point of building a website and getting ranked number one on Google?

Through lots of research, reading, and trial and error, I turned myself into a conversion rate optimization expert. It was not unusual for me to use conversion optimization tactics and persuasive copywriting to double or triple a client's leads and sales within forty-eight hours. Somehow, almost nobody was offering this miracle pill. When my partners and I started our own agency in 2007, we used this gap in the industry to create a unique service mix that worked like a charm to acquire new clients.

Here was my elevator pitch:

> "We're a digital marketing agency that does two things. We drive traffic to our clients' websites from pay-per-click advertising AND we help them convert that traffic to leads and sales by improving the website's user experience and content. Most agencies drive traffic to your site but don't know how to help you convert that traffic to leads and sales. Also, most web designers know how to make things look pretty but not how to design sites that sell."

I'm pretty sure we were, if not the first, one of the first agencies in the world talking about traffic generation AND conversion optimization together. That's what I like to call the milk-and-cookies approach to internet marketing.

Because we offered a unique mix of complementary services (including one service that was unique in and of itself), people wanted to talk to me and hire our agency. Prospects would say to me, "I've never heard any other agency talk about online marketing like that." We may not have been a cure for cancer, but we most definitely were not a generic brown box.

How can you offer a mix of services that make you unique to your ideal client? Is there a trend or gap in the industry you can fill with a "new" service? What services can you eliminate in order to seem like more of a specialist? What's different about your approach to a specific digital marketing tactic that's relevant to a particular audience?

Being a specialist (shortcut #1) can in and of itself be unique. But you can combine shortcuts, too. You can be a digital marketing specialist for software companies, for example, or you can take it a step further and be an SEO specialist for software companies.

SHORTCUT #3: PROVE YOU DELIVER BOTTOM-LINE RESULTS

There is an old marketing proverb that says, "People don't buy drill bits; they buy the holes that those bits can make." In other words, people don't buy the tool; they buy the result the tool delivers. But the original drill bit story does not go far enough. People don't want bits, and they don't want holes either. The hole is just a place to screw in a hook, and the hook is something on which they can hang their hat. So it's not the drill bit, the hole, or the hook that people want. They want a place to hang their hat.

Similarly, your prospects don't want social media. They don't even want fans or followers. Not really. What they really want is more money (leads and sales). They just assume the services (drill bits) they're asking for will result in more sales. Earlier in this chapter, I talked about how a customer has to believe you can produce profitable results. But that's not enough. At some point, you have to actually deliver those results.

If you can consistently use the services you offer to produce the end results your clients want and prove it to prospects during your sales presentation, you will have a superfast car and be positioned to win. There are a ton of snake oil salesmen in the internet marketing industry and many companies have been burned by previous agencies. As such, being able to prove (or better yet, guarantee) bottom-line business results is about as close to a cure for cancer as you're going to get.

The nuts and bolts of building and operating an agency that can produce profitable marketing outcomes for clients is beyond the scope of this book. That said, if you're positioning yourself to play Winnable Games, you're a good part of the way there. Here are a few key elements you should consider:

- Work with ideal clients and say no to everyone else.
- Have consistent, well-documented processes for delivering your services.
- Keep up with industry best practices.
- Hire A players who can deliver great work for your clients and teach the rest of your team.
- Create a company culture that attracts and retains top talent.

CLOSING THE LOOP: EVERYONE IS ON THE SALES TEAM

"Profit in business comes from repeat customers, customers that boast about your product or service, and that bring friends with them."

—W. EDWARDS DEMING

This chapter has been focused on helping you position your agency as the best choice. If you do that, attracting leads and closing deals will be significantly easier, even without a great sales system or ace closer. I want to cover one last point that will close the loop and create a virtuous cycle of sales success.

Everyone knows warm referrals close way easier than cold prospects. When a prospect reaches you via a referral from a happy client who got great results, the checkered flag is in view. You may be the only car in the race.

A virtuous cycle is a chain of events in which one positive outcome leads to another, which further promotes the first outcome and so on, resulting in a continuous process of improvement.

It's not uncommon, especially if you're selling high-priced services to sophisticated prospects, for them to ask for case studies and references before they sign your contract.

How can you have case studies to prove you do great work if your subject matter experts who work with the clients… you know…don't actually do great work? Similarly, you can't provide references if you don't have happy clients. Your agency must be committed to doing excellent work and producing great results so that clients sing your praises and refer new business your way. Even your administrative staff, such as the people in your billing department, can provide a positive or negative experience that colors a client's perception of your agency.

A sale is not a straight line from lead to closed deal that happens only within the sales department.

Instead, it's an integrated, virtuous cycle that encompasses your entire agency.

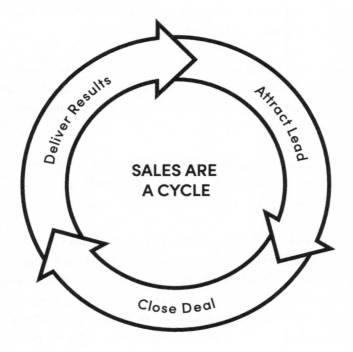

Great customer experiences, case studies, industry awards, references, and referrals don't come from your sales reps. They come from the rest of the people in your company. Nevertheless, they are a key part of your positioning, your marketing, and your sales team's chances to win deals. EVERYONE is on the sales team.

The good news is that if you've done all the positioning work covered in this chapter, your sales team will be providing your delivery team Winnable Games that lead to satisfied clients. That's how you retain clients and keep the virtuous cycle going.

The delivery team's excellent work can turn this client into a case study and
reference that can help win more deals down the road. Plus, their positive
experience may cause them to refer new clients to the agency.

Producing great results doesn't just get you referrals, testimonials, and references. It also gives your sales team rock-solid confidence in what they're promising during the sales process. And remember: Confidence. Closes. Deals.

EXAMPLE OF GREAT POSITIONING

By now, you should have a solid understanding of the importance of positioning and a bunch of specific ways to configure your agency to appear as the best choice. I want to end this chapter with an example of exactly what good positioning looks like.

A SAMPLE SALES SCENARIO THAT MATCHES AN IDEAL CLIENT PROFILE

A company that manufactures vacuum cleaners and traditionally sells them through big-box stores such as Home Depot and Lowe's is looking to start using the internet to sell directly to consumers. They have a nice website but no online marketing. They are interested in setting up a store on Amazon Marketplace.

Lump of Poop Positioning

"We're based in India and offer one hundred black hat SEO backlinks a month for $199."

Generic Brown Box Positioning

"We're a full-service digital marketing agency that's focused on producing results for our clients. We've been around for five years and have great customer service."

Pole Positioning

"We're a digital marketing agency that works exclusively with traditional manufacturers looking to sell their products directly to consumers. Not only do we specialize in working with manufacturers, but we are also laser focused on two services. We offer expert-level online advertising management and Amazon Marketplace consulting. Because of our unique focus and strict qualification criteria, our clients average a return on investment of ten times our fees, and we have the case studies to prove it."

Even though I used only a few of the positioning tools from this chapter and we have not even started discussing the actual sales system I'm going to teach you, the last agency is clearly the best choice and likely to win a lot of deals.

Obviously, not every sales scenario will be as perfect as the one I've laid out here, but if you use the positioning tactics in this chapter, you will ensure that your sales team is entering winnable races on a fast horse, not fishing in empty ponds or using the wrong bait.

The next chapter provides a high-level overview of the sales system you'll be building. I'll start by covering the mindset and philosophy that underpin the system. After that, I will describe each step so that you can visualize the entire blueprint.

KEY TAKEAWAYS FROM CHAPTER 2

- Take the time to position yourself ahead of your competitors and you'll win more deals more easily.

- You must differentiate your agency such that it's the best choice for at least one distinct type of customer.

- By identifying your ideal client profile(s), you'll set yourself up to play Winnable Games.

- Use the Fishing Framework to help you identify or create your Winnable Games.

- You can position your agency to win by agency type, service and pricing strategy, or specialization.

- Being able to prove you deliver bottom-line business results is the most powerful differentiator of all and the key to client retention.

- Everyone is on the sales team. Delivering great results for clients is the engine that powers your virtuous sales cycle.

CHAPTER 3

A BATTLE-TESTED BLUEPRINT

"Every well-built house started in the form of a definite purpose plus a definite plan in the nature of a set of blueprints."
—NAPOLEON HILL

MINDSET SHIFT: EAT WHAT YOU KILL IS SALES-LIMITING NONSENSE

I recently spoke to the owner of a boutique digital marketing agency who's had trouble hiring salespeople for years. He told me he was looking for a salesperson with an existing network who could generate new business on their own. In his mind, a salesperson should be able to generate most of their own leads, run the sales process, do all or most of the administrative work, close deals, and help onboard new clients. Essentially, he wants to hand someone a stack of business cards, release them into the wild, and have them come back with a feast.

I see owners of agencies (and many other businesses) do

this all the time. I call it the "eat what you kill" mindset. If you want to grow beyond a handful of new clients, that mindset is nonsense.

Another agency owner I worked with told me, "You know, I used to hire salespeople and expect them to generate their own leads and close deals. None of the people I hired ever generated enough sales. After a while, I realized it was unrealistic to find people that could do both tasks plus all the admin work and reach our sales goals. We're a marketing agency and we were not doing marketing for ourselves like we do for our clients. Once I shifted my mindset and expectations, everything changed. We started doing our own agency marketing to feed leads to the sales team. That freed them up to focus on actual selling, and growth took off like a rocket."

When I stepped into the sales role at my own agency, I took the lone-wolf approach. It seemed like there was no other choice. There were only three of us, and my partners were focused on taking care of the few clients we already had. Unless we wanted to raise a bunch of money (we didn't), I had to do it all. As I mentioned in the introduction, I grabbed a stack of business cards and took the $50-a-month "marketing budget" and got to work. And it worked. To a certain extent.

I was able to generate my own leads, run the entire sales process, and grow our agency to over seven figures. If you have limited resources and want to do the same thing, I'll show you the exact steps I took in the next chapter.

Even though it "worked," I was busy with so many tasks

that I could never consistently close more than one or two new deals for about $3,500–$5,000 in monthly fees. That was enough to hit our goals. However, if you have larger growth aspirations or want to avoid burnout, the macho "eat what you kill" approach is severely limiting both in terms of how many sales you can get out of each salesperson and in terms of whom you can hire. As I mentioned in chapter 1, having one person do everything and produce good results requires you to hire an expensive, multitalented sales unicorn.

Although it's perfectly fine to expect salespeople to generate some of their own leads, having your closers' lead-generation efforts be supplemental, rather than primary, means more sales per month and happier employees.

CORE METHODOLOGY: DIVIDE AND CONQUER WITH TEAM SELLING

Some people are great at marketing. Some people are great at cold calling. Some people are great at presenting and closing. And some people are well suited for the administrative side of sales. Very few people excel at all of those things. Even if you have a sales unicorn, the total number of new clients they can acquire will be limited.

One of the core philosophies of my approach to sales is to take a cue from McDonald's and break up the roles in your sales process. Have a few specialists running specific parts of the process, rather than one do-it-all short-order cook.

An agency hired me to handle sales and install the system you're learning in this book. The client had already done a great job with the positioning work we covered in chapter 2 and had one full-time marketing employee plus some third-party agencies in charge of generating leads. Besides lead generation, I had the support of other team members for the administrative parts of the process as well as the agency's subject matter experts to handle sales engineering (we'll cover what makes a great sales engineering process in chapter 7).

With team selling firmly embraced, instead of closing one or two deals a month, I was closing five to six deals for a total of $20,000–$45,000 in new recurring monthly revenue, plus lucrative one-time projects. We had so many leads coming in because of our excellent positioning, marketing, and client results that I pretty much never left the office or handed out a business card. I was just on the phone all day long fielding warm inbound leads and closing deals. Sales were at least 5X what I had done as a lone wolf.

As you go through the steps and stages outlined in this chapter, you'll start to see the various roles emerge. Although we're going to cover more than three roles, I encourage you to divide your system into at least the following three areas:

1. Lead generation
2. Core sales process
3. Administrative tasks that support the system

If you're a freelancer or tiny agency that cannot commit more than one person to sales, I'll provide modifications to the team selling philosophy in chapter 12. For now, even if only in your head, internalize the three roles as fits your situation.

CORE METHODOLOGY: AUTHENTIC, STRATEGIC SELLING

"Most people think 'selling' is the same as 'talking.' But the most effective salespeople know that listening is the most important part of their job."

—ROY BARTELL

In my opinion, just because someone contacts you and says they want Instagram advertising does not mean you should sell it to them. What that prospect is really saying is, "I want more sales, and I believe advertising on Instagram will get them for me." They may be totally wrong.

Since digital marketing is still relatively new, many prospects don't really know what they need, and they rarely ask for "more sales" directly. It's just assumed that whatever service they asked for will magically produce more sales at some point. Maybe it will; maybe it won't.

The best agency salespeople are sales strategists, not order takers or used car salesmen. Don't "sell" a prospect. Take a strategic approach to helping them solve their digital marketing problems.

Everything you do should be founded on authenticity and transparency. Just as you expect a doctor to give you the correct diagnosis, even if it's bad news, you should strive to provide prospects your best strategies for achieving their marketing goals. Don't blindly pitch a prospect on the service they asked for unless you believe the service is strategically sound.

Furthermore, strategic selling is about making sure the client purchases *all* the right services they need to achieve their business goals and *nothing else*. If you know they need three different marketing tactics that work together in order to hit their goals, even if you don't offer all three services, you need to give them the entire picture. If a doctor knows you need surgery AND physical therapy, it's malpractice to do the surgery and not mention the need for physical therapy.

Don't sell incomplete solutions or services people don't really need just because they asked for them. Be a strategic partner with the prospect. Explore their needs and options in a transparent, comprehensive, and authentic manner.

Here are the steps you can take to sell strategically (rather than transactionally):

1. Pinpoint and clarify the prospect's problems as they see them.
2. Identify the prospect's specific measurable goals or desired outcomes.
3. Diagnose the root cause(s) of the stated problems.
4. Propose the best strategic solution to get a prospect to their stated goals as efficiently as possible, regardless of what services they initially contacted you about.

I'll show you exactly how to sell strategically in chapters 6 and 7, where I cover the diagnosis and prescription processes in detail.

CORE METHODOLOGY: VALUE-BASED SELLING

You are not selling widgets. You are not selling hours. You are not selling packages. You are not selling "the lowest price." You are not even selling digital marketing. You are selling the value the prospect will receive if they become a client.

If a prospect had to pick, would they rather have three blog posts a month or three new clients at a profitable acquisition cost?

Don't ever forget what your client is really buying.

Your approach to sales and the messages you send to prospects should be determined by the value you will provide, not the list of tasks and deliverables in your proposal. It's not that the scope of work or number of hours you may be offering are not relevant, but they are not more important than bottom-line business results. The results are what you're selling, whereas the scope of work is how you're going to deliver those results. Lead by selling the value of the results, not the scope of work.

Okay, now let's look at all the steps and stages in the Clone the Ace Sales System so you have a clear picture of all the roles and functions you or your sales team need to be able to execute.

THE STEPS AND STAGES

The Clone the Ace Sales System has seven steps and eight deal stages. Although there is some overlap, the steps relate to the top-level elements of the entire *sales system*, from attracting leads all the way through to onboarding a new client. The deal stages, on the other hand, are specific to the core *sales process* and indicate the current status of each deal in your pipeline.

To make sure you are clear about the differences between steps and stages, let's use McDonald's as an example.

As I said earlier in the book, McDonald's is essentially a system designed to deliver inexpensive food quickly. When someone enters a McDonald's (step 1), they may be greeted by the person at the counter (step 2), who then asks the guest what they'd like to order (step 3). Once the order is entered into the ordering system (step 4), the cooks start preparing the food (step 5). The food preparation process is like our sales process and the point at which the stages begin. So, in our McDonald's example, the food preparation stages might be:

1. Order pending
2. Cooking started
3. Cooking complete
4. Food bagged
5. Customer served

Preparing the food is one, high-level step in the overall McDonald's system, while the stages indicate the status of how far along the customer's order is within the food preparation step.

In the sales system you'll be building, once a prospect has reached out and indicated they are ready to "order" some marketing and you've determined they are qualified enough to begin the formal sales process, the deal stages kick in.

We're going to cover the system steps at a high level here. In part two of the book, each step has its own chapter in which I cover the details. References to the stages are sprinkled throughout the book and become truly important when I cover tracking in chapter 11.

THE SYSTEM STEPS

Step #1: Attract

When I ask agency owners what their number one pain point is, they'll often say they need more clients. When I dig deeper, it's often leads they lack. Obviously, you can't close deals if nobody wants to talk to you. If you've done the positioning work we covered in chapter 2, you're ready to start filling up your pipeline with leads. In the next chapter, we'll dive deep into how to attract both the right quality and the right quantity of leads.

Step #2: Respond

What do you do when someone raises their hand and says they'd like to talk to you about your services? Do you have a consistent, effective, and well-documented process for handling new inquiries? Does it follow best practices? If you're like most of my clients, you have some sort of process for responding to leads, but it's been developed by default rather than through conscious effort and it's probably not as efficient, effective, or consistent as it could be.

Step #3: Diagnose

As we've discussed, top sales aces are not order takers. They're more like sales doctors who take the time to truly understand the prospect's pain points and the root causes of their symptoms before prescribing treatment. The diagnosis process I'm going to teach you in chapter 6 is one of the most powerful steps of the system and the one that average agencies most often skip. It's a huge opportunity to solidify your position as the best option.

Step #4: Prescribe

As we talked about earlier in this chapter, you have to recommend what you think is the best strategy and set of services to help each prospect relieve their pain and achieve their goals. It's a strategic approach to selling that we can use only if we've taken the time to diagnose a prospect's problems and needs.

Step #5: Present

One of the biggest and most common mistakes I see agencies make in their sales process is doing a quick initial discovery call and then either making a proposal on that first call or emailing a proposal shortly thereafter. Not good. Unless you're selling $500 cookie-cutter services to small, unsophisticated prospects, never email a proposal. You present proposals. You don't email them off into the ether and let prospects engage in unsupervised thinking.

By this step, you've worked hard to position yourself, attract leads, and warm them up on the first call. Don't blow it by rushing out a generic proposal focused only on the scope of work and the price. Ace closers present strategic solutions in an educational manner that drives home their agency's unique advantages and the value of their services.

ACE IN THE HOLE

If you currently email proposals after a quick intro call, you can immediately differentiate your agency and dramatically increase your chances of closing deals by taking the extra step of putting together a thoughtful proposal and presenting it in person or via web conference.

In chapters 8 and 9, I'm going to teach you how to easily create visually appealing presentations and present them in a way that will convince your prospects that hiring anyone else would be pretty stupid.

Step #6: Close

Coffee's for closers. ABC: Always. Be. Closing. Would you like delivery in October or November (said to a prospect who has not yet stated they want to hire you)?

Yes, there are closing techniques and skills you'll want to learn. However, these tired sales clichés need to be retired. In chapter 10, I will provide detailed strategies for closing deals in a way that won't make you feel like you need to take a shower after the contract is signed. Spoiler alert: It's about *inviting* the *right* people to enter into a *mutually beneficial relationship*, rather than tricking them into throwing their money down the drain.

Step #7: Onboard

A detailed discussion about onboarding processes is beyond the scope of this book, but it's an important part of the overall sales process. When a prospect signs a contract, they are excited but also shitting their pants. Until you actually deliver some results that prove they made the right choice, they will remain nervous and skittish. Having an organized process of handing clients off to your delivery team is a great first step in calming their nerves.

At a high level, you simply need to create a few processes and a checklist or two to make sure client expectations are clearly communicated to the delivery team and nothing falls through the cracks during this critical time in your new relationship. You've built trust; be sure to maintain it with a smooth transition.

THE DEAL STAGES

As I mentioned earlier, deal stages begin after a person has indicated they want to speak with your agency. The stages are the "labels" that indicate the current status of each deal in your sales pipeline. Even though all of the stages are critical, you can adjust them to your needs. We'll cover customizations in chapter 12.

Stage #1: Lead or Market Qualified Lead (MQL)

People define leads in several ways. Some people call the people who signed up for their email list leads. Some people consider a list of tradeshow attendees (whether they spoke to them at the show or not) leads. In the Clone the Ace system, leads have a very specific definition.

Said simply, a lead is a person who has expressly stated that they are interested in speaking with you about purchasing your services. This communication must be from a real person who's shopping for digital marketing services. At this stage, it does not matter if they're asking for services you don't offer or seem unqualified for some other reason (e.g., their budget is too small). We're simply determining whether they're an actual person looking for digital marketing (as opposed to a spambot or someone looking for a job).

Stage #2: Sales Qualified Lead (SQL)

SQLs are leads you've determined you want a salesperson to speak with. This is the stage where you use your ideal client profile to determine if the lead meets your basic criteria or if there are obvious disqualifiers. At this point, the lead is not fully qualified to receive a proposal; they're just qualified enough to have a diagnosis call with a sales rep.

Stage #3: Diagnosis Call Set

The next stage in our process is to set a call or face-to-face meeting to find out more about the prospect's needs and pain points. This is typically a thirty- to forty-five-minute meeting in which you will diagnose the situation and determine whether the prospect is qualified to work with your team. Why is simply setting a meeting (as opposed to actually having the meeting) a formal stage? You'll understand why in chapter 11, when I cover the tracking dashboard I recommend you use.

Stage #4: Diagnosis Call Complete

Similar to the last stage, we have a stage (mostly for tracking and troubleshooting purposes) that lets us know if the prospect actually showed up to the first meeting. If a prospect never shows up for a formal diagnosis call, they are by default not qualified. Even if they seemed perfect when the lead came in, we can't sell to people who won't speak with us.

Stage #5: Qualified/Preparing Proposal

During the diagnosis call, besides providing a bit of information about your agency to warm them up, you're going to be asking a lot of questions to help you determine if the prospect is qualified. If they are, they'll move on to the next stage. If not, you'll either end the conversation or refer them to someone else who can better meet their needs.

Stage #6: Proposal Presented

Once you decide someone is fully qualified, you create a formal proposal. The way you create and present proposals is another critical part of the process. It's not uncommon for people to say at the end, "That was the best presentation I've ever seen." I've even had prospects offer to pay me money just for the proposal presentation and many have sent me valuable thank-you gifts. I'll teach you how to achieve the same results in chapters 8 and 9.

Stage #7: Contract Sent

This is another tracking stage that helps with troubleshooting problems and forecasting sales. As with proposals and presentations, I have a specific way for you to create contracts that are efficient, flexible, and effective.

Stage #8: Closed Won/Closed Lost

Finally, tracking how many deals you've won or lost is key to closing the loop on your performance. Although it's listed as one stage here, for tracking purposes, you'd set this up as two different stages in your customer relationship management (CRM) system to place people in the correct bucket.

Now that you have a high-level overview of the system steps and deal stages, let's talk about a few more of the system's key ideas.

TASKS VERSUS SKILLS VERSUS KNOWLEDGE: WHOM SHOULD YOU HIRE TO DO SALES?

When I was simultaneously selling and delivering marketing services to clients, I often told people, "I'm not a real salesperson. I'm just a passionate practitioner who happens to sell the services, too." I was trying to point to the fact that I wasn't going to try to "sell" them but rather speak with them from a strategic standpoint.

There is an important difference between "sales skills" and knowledge about the services you're selling. Also, both skills and knowledge are different from the basket of tasks that support the sales process. Let's take a brief look at each, how they relate to your process and the type of people you might want to hire to run it.

TASKS

The task bucket contains the basic stuff that needs to get done to keep a lead moving through the pipeline. Examples of tasks are entering a lead into your CRM, setting meetings with a prospect, or reaching out to current clients to ask if they'd be a reference. Tasks tend to be more administrative in nature and rarely require advanced skills or deep industry knowledge. That said, sales engineering, building proposals, and presenting are more substantive tasks that do require some advanced skills.

SKILLS

The skills bucket contains the substantive selling behaviors that make someone an effective salesperson. Although the system I'm teaching you does a lot of the heavy lifting and allows you to hire average salespeople, those salespeople still need a solid level of skill in terms of active listening, written and verbal communication, and strategic thinking.

KNOWLEDGE

In any selling situation, knowing your products or services is essential to building credibility and convincing prospects you're offering the best solution to their problems. As you'll see in chapter 7, the Clone the Ace Sales System encourages you to have your subject matter experts (SMEs) help your sales team present your service offerings. It's another element of the system that relieves the pressure to hire sales unicorns.

That said, your SMEs will not be involved in the initial diagnosis call or most other parts of the sales process beyond the formal presentation. As such, your main salespeople need to understand the services you're selling deeply enough to speak intelligently during initial contact with the prospect. For example, if you sell SEO, your salespeople don't need to know the technical details of how to implement 301 redirects on a Magento website, but to make a good first impression, they do need to know what 301 redirects are and why they are important.

If you are going to hire a salesperson, looking for people who started their careers delivering internet marketing and managing clients before they got into sales can be an excellent option.

ACE IN THE HOLE

If you're taking a team selling approach, your salespeople don't need deep technical expertise. However, to make a good first impression and shepherd the deal through your entire sales process, sales professionals do need a solid understanding of internet marketing in general, how each service you offer works, what each service can and can't do, and how all of your services work together to produce results.

Your second option is to find an authentic, strategic salesperson who has at least some experience selling in the internet marketing industry, someone who understands how all your services work and fit together. They should also be open to learning your sales system.

Your last option is to hire a sharp, motivated person who has the right skills and mindset (authentic, personable, strategic thinker, etc.) and teach them about your services. If someone is a go-getter, pointing them to relevant online resources or even having them ride shotgun in client meetings can teach them to sound like they know what they're talking about.

The ideal client, type of agency, and service strategy you select dictates how knowledgeable your sales staff needs to be. Selling cookie-cutter services to unsophisticated small business owners takes less product knowledge than selling $10,000-a-month multiservice engagements to sophisticated marketing managers at large organizations.

SALES ENGINEERING: LET'S HEAR FROM THE EXPERTS

As you can see, there are quite a few steps, stages, and areas of skill needed for an effective, scalable sales system. That's why the team selling approach is so important. And one of the most important elements of the system is inserting your SMEs into the process. The idea behind sales engineering is that once you've determined that a prospect is fully qualified and you want to make a proposal, the SMEs conduct research relevant to the services up for discussion and present their findings and recommended strategy during the main sales presentation.

Instead of presenting a standard, static proposal, it's going to be an educational, eye-opening discussion that causes the prospect to say, "Wow, nobody else told me that, and it's clear you guys know what you're talking about." Generally, only SMEs doing the actual digital marketing work for clients day in and day out can get that sort of response from prospects, especially if the prospect is even a little bit knowledgeable about the services you're presenting.

I'm going to cover sales engineering more formally in chapter 7. For now, here are a few key reasons I recommend using sales engineers.

LET PROSPECTS TRY BEFORE THEY BUY

At the end of the day, you're selling your SMEs' ability to use the marketing tactics being considered to produce the client's desired results. The SMEs and their expertise are your product. If you were selling software, certainly the prospect would want a demo of the actual software. By including your SMEs in the presentation, you give the prospect a taste of what they're buying. If done right, it's far more persuasive to have an eight-year web development veteran explain your services than a salesperson who just knows the basics of coding.

IMPROVE CLIENT RETENTION

The second reason sales engineering is important is that you want to bring on ideal clients—clients you are confident you can help, such that they are happy, stick around, and refer you to others. By having one or more of your SMEs poke around the prospect's Google Ads and analytics accounts, for example, you're giving your team another opportunity to make sure the prospect represents a Winnable Game and that you are bringing on clients with whom success is nearly certain (recall our friends at the hospital I mentioned in chapter 2).

FIND GOLDEN NUGGETS TO HELP CLOSE DEALS

Sales engineering allows your team to uncover opportunities the client has and present an initial strategy for taking advantage of them. There are few things more persuasive in the sales process than educating a prospect on glaring issues in their account or low-hanging-fruit opportunities that other agencies have not shared. Also, doing a bit of free research allows you to scope and price your work accurately and create a clear roadmap for landing and retaining the client.

REDUCE PRESSURE ON YOUR SALES TEAM

The final benefit of using sales engineers is that it takes enormous pressure off your hiring process and the sales reps' day-to-day responsibilities. You're not going to find an experienced, competent salesperson who also has the same deep knowledge in all your service areas as the SMEs who are in the trenches developing, deploying, and managing digital marketing campaigns day in and day out. It's one less requirement you have to fill when hiring salespeople.

Okay, in part one of this book, I covered a variety of important concepts and strategies you can use to lay the foundation for sales success, and I provided an overview of the Clone the Ace Sales System. It's finally time to build and run your sales machine.

KEY TAKEAWAYS FROM CHAPTER 3

- Take a team selling approach so you're not relying on one person to handle every part of the process.

- Don't be an order taker. Sell authentically and strategically to ensure your clients are getting ALL the right services they need to achieve their business goals.

- Sell the value, not merely your time or a list of tasks.

- The Clone the Ace Sales System has seven steps and eight deal stages. Be sure your system covers all of them or has a good reason for skipping something.

- Insert sales engineers into your sales process to take pressure off your sales team and give your prospects a real taste of the expertise they are buying.

PART TWO

BUILD AND RUN YOUR SALES MACHINE

CHAPTER 4

ATTRACT THE LEADS YOU NEED

"Half the money I spend on advertising is wasted; the trouble is I don't know which half."

—JOHN WANNAMAKER

In 2018, HubSpot conducted a survey and asked, "What are your agency's biggest pain points?" Sixty percent of the respondents listed "finding new clients" as their number one problem.

WHAT ARE YOUR AGENCY'S BIGGEST PAIN POINTS?

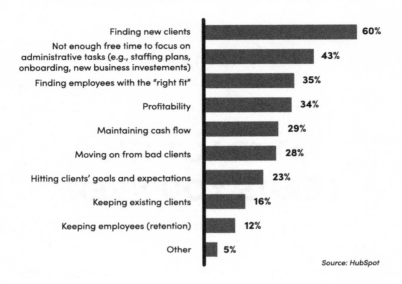

Finding new clients	60%
Not enough free time to focus on administrative tasks (e.g., staffing plans, onboarding, new business investements)	43%
Finding employees with the "right fit"	35%
Profitability	34%
Maintaining cash flow	29%
Moving on from bad clients	28%
Hitting clients' goals and expectations	23%
Keeping existing clients	16%
Keeping employees (retention)	12%
Other	5%

Source: HubSpot

When I speak with agency owners, sales managers, and freelancers, they often say the same thing. However, when I dig deeper, it becomes evident that the real problem is a lack of leads.

This indicates a phenomenon I've observed over the years: people know they need more sales, but they have a very hazy idea (or none at all) of what the actual problem is, let alone how to fix it. This is true not only of the agencies I work with but their clients, too.

ATTRACTING VERSUS GENERATING LEADS

Although I never do it, I'm not going to claim that cold calling is dead. Whether by phone, email, or old-fashioned door knocking, cold outreach can certainly generate leads and sales. But it's the least efficient way to do so. Most salespeople hate it and are not good at it. Also, prospects dislike being bothered, and cold outreach can damage your brand.

If your agency is so great, why do you have to bother people who are busy and mostly not shopping for your services? Rather than grinding out leads through blood, sweat, and tears, you want to attract them to you like a magnet.

Which lead would you rather handle?

GENERIC, COLD LEAD

One of your sales reps making a hundred calls a day gets lucky and reaches a business owner who just happens be in the market for digital services but has never heard of your agency. Nevertheless, simply because the rep has caught her on a good day, she reluctantly agrees to a rushed initial call.

TARGETED, WARM LEAD

The owner of an automotive parts store has recently seen the natural search rankings and traffic to his e-commerce store drop 30 percent. He's desperate to fix the rankings slide and get traffic back to previous levels.

To find a solution, he conducts a few Google searches and finds an article you wrote titled "How to Troubleshoot SEO Drops on E-Commerce Sites." The store owner finds the article well written and informative. He spends another ten minutes on your site checking out other articles and case studies. Because your content was so useful, he signs up for your email newsletter.

During his research, he notices that your agency specializes in e-commerce SEO. That gets him even more excited. He thinks you might have the solution to his problem and fills out a contact form to schedule a sales call.

Obviously, you want lead #2. Although the above example is just one way to attract leads, the point is that you want the core of your marketing strategy to be an attraction-based strategy, rather than predominantly a cold, grind 'em out approach.

DO YOU EVEN KNOW WHAT A PROBLEM IS, BRO?

One of the main reasons people are so confused about how to solve their sales problems is that they don't clearly understand the differences between symptoms, problems, causes, and solutions.

Let's use a simple medical example.

Your son is not feeling well, so you take him to the doctor. The nurse asks, "What's going on? What's the problem?" And you say, "My son has had a headache, a sore throat, and a cough for three days. It seems to be getting worse." Those aches and pains sound like a problem. They're not. Those are *symptoms* of a problem. When the doctor begins the examination, he's trying to find the problem that's *causing* the symptoms. After a bit of poking and prodding and a test, he declares that your son's problem is strep throat.

Now, before the doctor can prescribe the solution to your son's problem, he has to identify the root cause. The root cause of strep throat is a bacterial infection. The typical solution is to take antibiotics. If the root cause of the symptoms was instead a viral infection, the prescribed solution would be different because antibiotics don't heal viral infections.

Before you can solve your sales problems, you have to distinguish the symptoms from the problems from the root causes. Only then can you determine and implement the solution.

HOW TO DIAGNOSE AND SOLVE ANY SALES OR MARKETING PROBLEM

I'm going to teach you a process you can use to quickly eliminate confusion and accurately diagnose any sales or marketing problem. Although we're going to apply the process to your sales and marketing situation, it can be used on any problem in your life.

I assume you picked up this book because you have what I'd call common sales symptoms. When someone comes to me and says, "I need more clients," I start asking diagnostic questions, like a doctor, to better define the symptoms so I can zero in on the problems and root causes.

The reason this process is important is that making a general statement like "I'm not getting enough new clients" does not tell you what the actual problems or solutions may be. It's like telling a doctor you have a headache. There may be many causes of a headache, and she has to probe to find them. For example, here are four scenarios that all present as "not enough sales" but are really four totally different problems that may require four different solutions:

1. I'm getting two quality leads a month, but I need ten = lead volume issue
2. I'm getting ten leads a month, but they're mostly junk = lead quality issue
3. I'm getting two new clients a month, but I need five = sales volume issue
4. I'm getting five new clients a month, but they're mostly junk = sales quality issue

Start diagnosing your sales challenges by asking yourself, "Where exactly does it hurt?" As shown in the chart, there are only four possible answers.

	MARKETING	SALES
VOLUME	Not Enough Leads	Not Enough Deals
QUALITY	Poor Quality Leads	Poor Quality Deals

You may be experiencing pain in one, several, or all four of these areas. As you dig into your general sales pain by asking good diagnostic questions, you begin to get clarity on where you need to dig deeper and where the solutions to your specific sales challenges lie.

Since it's the problem I hear about most often, let's assume "not enough leads" is what you're dealing with. As we go through the example for lead volume, you'll see how you can apply the same process to the other three problems. Also, the rest of this book provides detailed solutions to the problems on the sales side of the chart, so you don't have to worry about those right now.

Okay, in this scenario, not getting enough revenue from new client acquisition is your main symptom (sore throat). Lack of lead volume is your main problem (strep). Next, you have to start looking for root causes. Why are you not getting enough leads? Again, there are only four possible answers.

THE FOUR ROOT CAUSES OF LEAD VOLUME ISSUES

Wrong Tactics	Poor Execution
Not Enough Effort	Business Issues

Let's look at the four options in turn and you will start to see the root cause(s) of your lead volume problem.

WRONG TACTICS

When you're using the wrong tactics, there's either a strategic mismatch between your marketing goals and your target prospects or a mismatch between your strategy and your skills or resources.

For example, let's say you're targeting the owners of accounting practices. Advertising on Snapchat, which is used mainly by eighteen- to twenty-four-year-olds who are not accountants, is the wrong tactic. Are you fishing in the ponds your prospects are swimming in? If not, you may be using the wrong tactics.

Looking at this from another angle, public speaking can be a great lead attraction tactic but not if you hate speaking and are unwilling to develop effective speaking skills.

Just because a tactic is strategically sound does not mean it's right for you.

POOR EXECUTION

Now let's assume you are using tactics that are strategically appropriate, but they're still not working well. Your lack of leads may be due to flawed execution of the tactic.

Let's say your agency offers web design and content marketing services. You've decided to use Google Ads to generate leads (strategically sound). However, because you're not a paid search expert, you make mistakes in your campaign setup that negatively impact your results. This is an example of poor tactical execution.

Note that once you get to the tactical level, there are deeper layers of diagnosis needed. In our paid search example, you would need to ask, "What specifically about my paid search campaigns is not set up correctly? Is it the ad copy, the keywords I'm using, the landing pages, or a combination of all three?" And if you identify that the ad copy is the problem, what specifically about it is wrong? Asking those questions is how you get to the very bottom of an issue to see its root cause.

If you're using a tactic that should be working but isn't, there is either a problem with your execution or with the amount of effort you're giving the tactic.

NOT ENOUGH EFFORT

Here, I'm referring to the time and money you apply to a

tactic. I'm also referring to the number of tactics you're using (e.g., you're using only one lead generation tactic when you should be using two or three).

Here are a few examples.

You want to generate ten leads a month. Every time you go out and speak, you attract five leads. But you speak only once per month and you don't do anything else to attract leads. I actually had the owner of a very successful agency present this scenario to me.

One of the owners of that agency is a well-known speaker in the digital marketing industry. His partner called and told me they were not consistently generating enough leads. Some months they'd get a bunch of great leads, and other months they'd get very few. He then said, "When [famous person] goes out and speaks, we get a lot of leads." So I asked if the famous person was speaking every month. The answer was, "No. He might speak five or six times over two to three months and then not speak at all for a few months."

Well, the solution is pretty simple. The tactic of speaking is strategically appropriate and well executed, as evidenced by the fact that every time the famous person speaks, he generates a good number of quality leads. It's just not being applied consistently. There is not enough effort/ time being spent to produce consistent results.

Some tactics require a certain amount of money to work well. Let's say you want to use paid online ads to generate one lead per day. Your analytics tells you that it takes ten clicks on your ads for you to generate one lead and each click costs $5. In this scenario, if you have a daily budget that is less than $50, you can't hit your daily lead generation goal.

Other tactics require a certain amount of time before they work well, SEO being an obvious example. If you're doing content marketing and SEO for your own agency, you can't write three blog posts and declare after a month it's not working. Although it's possible to write a hit article that generates a bunch of action straight away, it's also pretty rare. Generally, content marketing takes a sustained effort for at least four or five months before you start seeing traction. Similarly, if you use TV or radio advertising, it takes many exposures for viewers to remember your ads and take action. You can't run one radio commercial or go to one networking event and make an informed decision about whether the tactic is working or not.

Another issue related to marketing effort is the number of tactics and marketing channels you use.

One of my clients had done content marketing and got themselves on the MOZ list of recommended agencies. When I first started working with them, nearly 70 percent of their leads and sales were coming from that list. The other 30 percent would trickle in mostly from word of mouth. Because the owner had aggressive growth goals, he realized he needed to diversify his lead sources. After all, he had no control over the MOZ list and his listing could go away at any time. Plus, there was nothing he could do to get more leads from the MOZ list. It was generating a certain number of leads and that was that.

On a mission to diversify, we added a microsite for one of the agency's core services paired with highly targeted paid search ads. Also, the CEO hired a top-notch content marketing agency, had his own SEO team focus more on their website, and invested in a booth at several large trade shows. A year later, sources were diversified and leads were growing in volume. The new lead sources came online just in the nick of time as Rand Fishkin left MOZ in 2018 and the leads flowing in from the list all but dried up.

A related issue is that some agencies fail to use complementary tactics. For example, if you use paid social ads, you should probably also use remarketing. Creating and optimizing the user experience on targeted landing pages also has a major impact on the effectiveness of paid ads. The point is that some tactics work best when paired with others. If you're using only one of three tactics that depend on each other, your results will be less than optimal.

Are you applying enough time and money to your tactics? Do you understand how to implement the tactics correctly? Are you clear about how long each tactic takes to mature, or are you making hasty decisions and cutting campaigns too soon? Are you using too few or too many tactics? Are your marketing campaigns missing any complementary tactics?

BUSINESS ISSUES

Diagnosing and solving business issues is easily an entire other book. That said, it's critical we touch on business issues because if you are dealing with one or more of the examples below, nothing you do with your marketing tactics will solve your lead attraction problem.

Let's start with an example that relates more to your prospects than to your agency, because that's a more straightforward way to introduce the concept. We'll then look at a few agency-specific business issues you may have.

Let's say your client Joe Schmo owns a small e-commerce website that resells basic cotton T-shirts made by Hanes. Their site offers the T-shirts for $12.00 each plus a $5.00 shipping fee. The same T-shirt from Hanes is available on Amazon.com for $10.00 each with free two-day shipping. Unless a person is simply unaware of the better deal on Amazon, nobody should buy a shirt from Joe Schmo. Better marketing can't fix this issue. It's a fundamental flaw in the business model.

amazon

$10.00
+ Free Shipping with Prime

Joe Schmo's T-Shirt Shack

$12.00
+ $5.00 Shipping

Here are a few examples of business issues I see at digital marketing agencies that make it hard to attract leads (and close deals).

They're Not Very Good

The agency is simply not very good at the digital marketing it offers. As a result, the agency can't point to many (or any) positive case studies or provide references.

They're behind the Times

The agency offers services that are outdated or in weak demand.

They're Stuck in the Hamster Wheel of Death

A freelancer or small agency without a dedicated salesperson puts in the effort to get a few clients, then becomes so busy taking care of those clients that they neglect their own marketing. Later, when they lose a client or two and need more business, their pipeline is dry. They have to start lead generation all over again. Exhausting and stressful! I know, I've been there.

They Look like a Poor Option

The agency's service fees are higher than their competitors' fees with no obvious additional value offered to justify the price. Or their prices are so low their ideal clients don't believe they're any good.

They're Fishing in an Empty Pond

They are offering services to an industry that is dying or too small, making attracting enough leads nearly impossible. I have a client that sells software to the book publishing industry. No matter what he tries to do to generate leads, there just are not very many fish in the pond, as the book publishing industry continues to get smaller and smaller each year.

They Lack Differentiation and Value

They did a poor job with positioning and branding such that they do not offer any obvious unique value to any specific target market.

As you can see, your problem, not enough leads, may have one or more root causes that are manifesting as your symptom of "not enough sales." You must first identify the root cause by checking your situation against the frameworks presented in this section. Only then can you start prescribing and implementing solutions. Answer the three questions below, and the rest of this chapter will show you how to develop the right lead attraction solution.

1. What are my symptoms?
2. What are the main problems?
3. What are the root causes of each problem?

By the way, this entire diagnosis framework will work for your clients, too. You can and should apply this exact approach during the diagnosis phase of the sales process. I'll teach you why and exactly how to do that in chapter 6.

THREE-WHEEL MARKETING AND HOW TO MAKE INFINITY PER HOUR

Now that you know why you're not generating enough leads, you have to figure out how to address the root causes and solve your marketing problems so you can have a steady stream of qualified prospects flowing through your sales system.

As we discussed in the last section, you don't want to have too few or too many tactics. If you have too few, you may not attract enough leads and risk relying too heavily on one tactic, which may stop producing leads at any time.

Freelancers and small-to-midsize agencies should typically use two to five tactics. Use more than that and you risk stretching your resources too thin. It's better to have two or three tactics working well than eight barely carrying their weight. You can always add more later.

ACE IN THE HOLE

Don't fall into the marketing hype hole. You don't need to be on all sixteen hot social media platforms, write eight blog posts a week, and advertise on blimps and bus stop benches to be successful. It's much more effective to execute one or two tactics really well than to spread your resources (time and money) across too many at once.

So what tactics should you use? That depends on your goals, your positioning, and available resources (time, skill, and money).

To help you begin to frame the right lead attraction strategy, I'd suggest you pick one tactic in each of the following three areas. I call them Marketing Wheels.

FLYWHEELS

Here is the dictionary definition of a flywheel from Google:

> Noun. A heavy revolving wheel in a machine that is used to increase the machine's momentum and thereby provide greater stability *or a reserve of available power* during interruptions in the delivery of power to the machine.

Said simply, a flywheel is a part of a machine that stores energy the machine can use to generate results when the main energy source is not available.

In marketing, a flywheel is something you initially put energy into (sometimes a lot of energy), but once it's up and running, it takes little to no energy to maintain. SEO is an example. You have to put a lot of energy into acquiring top rankings for highly searched and relevant keywords, but once you're well ranked, you don't necessarily have to keep up the same level of effort to produce traffic and leads over the long term.

Another example would be the MOZ list of recommended agencies I mentioned earlier. Initially, my client worked hard producing content and establishing a relationship with Rand Fishkin. But once they got on the coveted list, the leads flowed in for many years with almost no effort. Strategic referral partnerships with complementary agencies are another type of flywheel.

Working toward getting at least one flywheel set up is a worthy endeavor.

MONEY WHEELS

Money Wheels are similar to flywheels in that they are tactics that, once you put energy into them, spit out leads somewhat automatically. The difference is that the energy you put in is in the form of money, instead of time and effort. Another difference is that you generally have to keep putting in the same amount of money for as long as you use the tactic.

Paid online advertising is a Money Wheel. So is having a booth at a tradeshow. Despite the ongoing cost, Money Wheels can be a powerful part of your total lead attraction strategy in that you can use the leverage of money to free up your time to take care of your clients, do other marketing, run your business, or sit on your ass and drink beer.

It's usually a good idea to have at least one Money Wheel in your mix. After all, if you're an agency selling digital marketing services, you are basically in the Money Wheel business. Unlike drug dealers, you should use some of your own products to attract leads.

HAND CRANKS

The third type of Marketing Wheel is a Hand Crank. These are manual in nature. Networking and speaking at conferences are two examples of tactics that require a human being's continued time and effort. Like that famous agency speaker I mentioned earlier, if you stop speaking, the leads from speaking will stop.

Besides attracting leads, some Hand Cranks get you out of the office and face-to-face with your prospects, potential partners, and competitors so you can keep your finger on the pulse of your industry.

ACE IN THE HOLE

Hand Cranks, when used correctly, can turn into flywheels. For example, speaking might generate direct leads, but it could also lead to strategic partnerships that refer warm leads to your agency indefinitely.

The three wheels overlap and intersect. For example, SEO can be a flywheel, but it's sort of a Hand Crank at the beginning when you have to create a lot of content. Alternatively, you can execute SEO as a Money Wheel by paying an SEO agency to do it for you and have it turn into a flywheel down the road. Regardless of the crossover, the framework is still a useful way to distinguish different types of tactics and make sure you have at least one of each (if you have a larger agency with enough resources to do more than three things well, by all means, go for it).

Just remember, you must pick the right tactics from a strategic standpoint, execute them well, and apply the appropriate level of effort for them to attract the leads you need.

BONUS: MAGIC WHEELS

A few years ago, I started an engagement with a new client, and one of the first things I noticed was that the owner, who was running sales by himself and was completely underwater, had auto emails going out to every form submission that came through his website. The autoresponders were his way of filtering out tire kickers. Not a bad idea and totally necessary in some situations.

However, when you're overwhelmed, filtering can become too heavy-handed and you can end up throwing the baby out with the bath water. This agency owner was handling sales by himself because, like many other agency owners, he'd tried to hire salespeople in the past but was always disappointed with the results. So he felt like he had no choice but to do it himself and use a heavy-handed filter.

When I started working with his agency, I had him immediately remove the autoresponders. I was responsible for fielding leads, and I wanted to get a sense of what was coming through the front door before I refined the qualification process.

Simultaneously, I set up a few referral commission agreements with reputable agencies. These relationships allowed me to forward unqualified leads and earn commissions for my client. Simply by talking to more prospects, we won more deals, and we were able to refer out several leads per week. After a year, we'd received nearly $20,000 in referral commissions (it was almost zero the year before).

I walked into the owner's office and relayed the good news. He was familiar with the three Marketing Wheels and said, "That's awesome. What kind of wheel is that?" I replied that it was a Magic Wheel. We took leads that were being thrown into the garbage and simply forwarded them to our referral partners and made a bunch of money. Although there is obviously some cost to generating the leads in the first place, his hourly rate on that referral revenue was basically infinity, and the money continues to roll in to this day with no additional work.

ACE IN THE HOLE

Another example of a Magic Wheel is a static product, such as an online course that teaches people to do what you do for your clients. You can sell the course to prospects who don't qualify to work with you directly and deliver it with minimal maintenance.

Bottom line: While you're setting up your Marketing Wheels, throw in a Magic Wheel or two. A year from now, you can thank me for the "free money" flowing into your bank account.

THE BEST LEAD ATTRACTION STRATEGIES FOR AGENCIES

Below are several marketing strategies and tactics that tend to work well for digital agencies. The list is not exhaustive or in any particular order. It's meant as a quick-start guide. Mix, match, and add marketing tactics as you see fit.

- Content marketing
- Strategic/referral partnerships
- Trade shows and conferences

- Paid search and social advertising with targeted landing pages and microsites
- Public speaking
- Webinars
- SEO
- Online and offline networking
- Email marketing
- Public relations
- ABM (account-based marketing)

THE EXACT PLAN I USED TO CREATE A SEVEN-FIGURE AGENCY STARTING WITH A $50-A-MONTH MARKETING BUDGET

In the introduction, I told the story of how I took over sales for my fledgling agency and grew revenues to over seven figures with nothing more than a stack of business cards and fifty bucks a month. People often ask me what I did with only $50. Below is the exact plan I used:

1. Go to four networking events per month.
2. Speak at least once per month.
3. You can do more, but never do less.

I had the plan written down on my task list just like I wrote it above. The $50 was basically for parking and entrance fees to networking events.

Let me explain why it worked. It's obviously not because it's an exotic, brilliant plan.

POLE POSITIONING

As I discussed earlier, we had excellent positioning. At the time, we were one of, if not the only agency offering world-class paid online advertising services combined with conversion rate optimization. I developed a killer elevator pitch around that unique combination which hooked people instantly.

PASSION AND ENERGY

I was super passionate about what we were doing, and my enthusiasm came through during my networking and speaking.

CONSISTENCY

There were many months when I did more than four networking events and spoke more than once. But there was NEVER, EVER a month, for four or five years straight, when I did less than the minimum. My effort was consistent.

I truly ran around town like a nutjob with my hair on fire, going to any event I could find, even the lame meetups with three people in a coffee shop discussing the movie *The Secret*. Eventually, I refined my strategy so I was spending more time at better quality events.

The main point is that I put in the time month in, month out.

I got good at things I disliked. I was not a social butterfly. I HATED networking and, like most people, was terrified of public speaking. However, my desire to make our agency successful was stronger than my fear. So I read books, I studied, I practiced, and I forced myself to get good at networking and speaking. Unexpectedly, the tactics I once hated became fun, and I'm now a professional speaker (not-so-subtle hint: you can hire me to speak at your event; visit www.solvesales.com for more information).

The hard work paid off. Over time, we were able to increase our budget and expand our reach. Through my networking and speaking (Hand Cranks), we secured clients and referral partners who sent us leads for years (flywheels).

During this period, I was invited to join a national speaking tour which had me presenting at large marketing conferences all over the United States about twice a week. Because we were doing well, we had no issue expanding our budget to pay for my travel. As we grew, we invested additional funds into building a microsite and launching targeted paid search traffic to it (Money Wheel). Because we were picky with qualifying prospects and did excellent work that produced tangible business results for our clients, we started getting referrals from clients, too (another flywheel).

I've included this story and plan in the book not necessarily because I recommend you do the same thing but to emphasize that you can start like I did and still be successful. I had no experience selling digital marketing, empirical evidence from my former boss that I sucked at sales, a strong dislike for networking and speaking, and basically no budget. And it still worked.

Although this chapter and this story are mostly about marketing, it's really about the entire point of the book. I've worked my ass off figuring out how to attract leads and sell. And this book is my way of giving back to all my brothers and sisters slogging it out in the trenches. My hope is that you don't have to spend seventeen years perfecting your approach. You can use this book to clone me and take some major shortcuts to marketing and sales success.

DEFINING YOUR DESTINATION: CREATING THE RIGHT LEAD ATTRACTION STRATEGY FOR YOUR AGENCY

"If you don't know where you're going, any road will take you there."

—LEWIS CARROLL (*ALICE IN WONDERLAND*)

Before I end this chapter, I want to address one of the first questions I ask every prospect. To efficiently fix your lead attraction problems, you have to answer it.

What is your specific, measurable goal?

If your goal is to generate ten leads a month from small local retail businesses, you might decide on a marketing strategy that includes attending events at your local chamber of commerce and setting up a $500-a-month paid search campaign geotargeted to your city.

If, on the other hand, your goal is to generate fifty leads

a month from larger, national businesses, you're going to need a totally different mix of tactics, resources, and skills.

Make sure you're clear on your destination before you lock down your lead attraction strategy.

By now, you've done a ton of work. You've positioned your agency to win. You've learned the core steps and stages of the sales system. You've diagnosed your lead attraction issues and begun to fill your pipeline with hot prospects. It's finally time to sell! Let's dig into each step in the system and learn the sales skills that pay the bills.

KEY TAKEAWAYS FROM CHAPTER 4

- Although prospecting can be an important tactic, it's more effective to have a lead attraction approach.

- The first step in addressing your marketing and sales challenges is to accurately diagnose the symptoms, problem(s), and root causes.

- Use a mix of flywheels, Money Wheels, and Hand Cranks to attract the leads you need.

- Set up Magic Wheels to earn referral commissions on leads that don't fit your ideal client profile.

- You don't need a big budget to be successful. You just need to skillfully and consistently execute the right tactics.

- Setting specific, measurable marketing and sales goals is the first step to creating the right lead attraction strategy for your agency.

- It's much better to have two or three marketing tactics working well than to overextend your resources trying to execute all of the hot marketing tactics of the moment.

CHAPTER 5

LEAD RESPONSE THAT PUTS YOU IN THE LEAD

"If everything seems under control, you're not going fast enough."

—MARIO ANDRETTI

SPEED SELLS

If you attempt to contact a web lead within five minutes of receiving it, your odds of getting the prospect on the phone are one hundred times greater than if you wait just thirty minutes. Furthermore, your chances of qualifying that lead to enter your formal sales process are twenty-one times greater. Wait over an hour and the stats drop off an even larger cliff. Speed sells.[4]

---

4   Michael Pendreigh, "3 Response Time Studies: Lead Generation & Wasted Sales Leads," Business2Community.com, June 28, 2016, https://www.business2community.com/ sales-management/3-response-time-studies-lead-generation-wasted-sales-leads-01580290.

As we've learned, pole positioning lets you start the race from the front of the pack. Using the right strategies for responding to leads can solidify your position at the top of a prospect's list before you even get to the formal presentation.

If you use Gmail, you know that when an email arrives, the system shows the time it came in. It starts off at zero minutes and then counts up as time goes by until it eventually changes to the date the email was sent. Because responding to leads quickly is so important, I like to play a little game with myself and try to respond, either by email or phone, when the time counter still says zero minutes.

When I call prospects within a minute or so of them submitting a web form, it freaks them out—in a good way. It's so unusual that I've differentiated myself before even saying a word. Also, getting back to clients quickly conveys that your agency is responsive, which is a HUGE deal in an industry with a reputation for crappy client communication.

Obviously, you have other responsibilities and you can't monitor your inbox twenty-four hours a day. Do your best. The data does not lie. Speed, throughout the sales process, especially when it comes to initial lead response, helps increase contact and qualification rates while creating and maintaining momentum.

If lead volume and your overall sales responsibilities prevent you from responding to leads quickly, it's time to get some support. Whether it's time to hire an administrative assistant or contract with a third party to handle initial lead response, it's critical that you pay attention to this part of the process and find a solution that works for you. However you do it, do it. It's that important. By itself, quick lead response can bag you a substantial amount of extra deals each year.

For example, I used to forward the same unqualified leads to two referral partners (Magic Wheels). One of them would respond to the prospect instantly, whereas the other one might take a day or two to respond. The quick responder closed almost all the referrals. The slow responder kept complaining that the leads were not closing. Go figure.

The same goes for all other parts of the sales process. If you promise to send someone a case study or a reference, get it done as quickly as possible.

Should you respond via email or phone? When you can, responding to leads by phone is preferable. If someone fills out a form on your website and they get a call from a real person two or three minutes later, they won't even believe it. However, if you don't have time to talk at that moment, you can either call to set up the diagnosis meeting for a later date or you can still get very good results responding by email, as long you do it quickly.

Although I don't have a lot of experience with automated chatbots and don't believe email autoresponders have the same impact as personal outreach, they are at least worth testing. Some response shortly after initial contact is better than no response for twelve hours.

WHOA! WHOA! WHOA! SLOW DOWN, BUDDY

"It is a mistake to think that moving fast is the same as actually going somewhere."

—STEVE GOODIER

Although speed sells, it's also true that haste makes waste. Once you get a prospect on the phone, it's time to slow down and be a bit more thoughtful. Sales is like dating. You don't ask someone to marry you five minutes after you've met them. You have to build rapport, trust, and mutual understanding first. Even though rapport can and should be built pretty quickly, trust takes longer.

Many agencies, especially ones that sell low-end, cookie-cutter services, tend to want to have a quick first call, collect a bit of information, and send out a standard proposal ten minutes later. Although that may work in certain circumstances (think Yelp selling a $250-a-month paid advertising program on their review platform), it's absolutely the wrong approach if you want to sell $15,000 app development or $5,000-a-month social media programs.

In the Clone the Ace Sales System, there are steps that you take to set yourself up for success. These may require you to slow down your current process. If you do, you'll get two important benefits:

1. Taking the time to really understand a prospect's needs and goals allows you to be more discriminating when you're qualifying them. This can help filter out problem clients and protect your team's morale.
2. If you take the time to build trust and use the diagnosis process I'll teach you in the next chapter, the prospect

will give you the key information you need to create a winning proposal.

Go fast on the administrative parts of your sales process and slow down the substantive parts. You'll avoid mistakes and close more deals.

Here are all the steps to ace level lead response:

1. Quickly sales qualify the lead. Do they meet basic criteria to speak with a salesperson?
2. Contact SQLs within five minutes to set up a thirty- to forty-five-minute diagnosis call.
3. Enter or update the lead record in your CRM system.
4. Schedule the diagnosis call and send a calendar invite to the prospect.
5. If the call is scheduled for a day and time in the future, send a reminder email (preferably an automated template) six to twelve hours before the call.
6. Conduct a kickass diagnosis call using the techniques I'll show you in the next chapter.
7. If the prospect is fully qualified, begin the sales engineering process I'll cover in chapter 7.

As the first bullet point indicates, we don't want to waste time setting up meetings with people who are obviously not a match for our services. Also, if we have a lot of leads, we want to make sure we match the right sales resources and level of priority/effort to the opportunity. That's where screening and lead scoring come in.

PRESCREENING TIRE KICKERS

If you have more leads than your current sales staff can handle, you can of course hire more sales resources. However, if you don't want to hire more people at this time or feel you have too many low-quality leads coming in the door, you may choose to implement a prescreening process that prospects have to go through before you offer a diagnosis call. There are a few ways you can do it. Here are two simple ones.

EMAIL SCREENING

Your first email response to a lead can include two or three comments and qualifying questions that they have to respond to before you'll set up a diagnosis call. This email can be automated to go out to every lead or sent manually using a quickly customizable template. However you do it, making it sound as natural and customized as possible is important. Here is an example:

[First Name]

Thanks for reaching out to our agency about content marketing. To determine if we're a good fit for each other, we'll need to set up an initial discovery call so I can find out more about your specific situation.

To make sure it's a good use of our time, I wanted to let you know that our fees for content marketing range from $3,500 to $10,000 per month and work best when at least one person on your team is available to meet weekly to discuss the content calendar, review topic ideas, give feedback on drafts, etc.

Does that budget level and time requirement sound like a good fit to you?

Also, would you mind providing a sentence or two describing what's happening in your business right now that caused you to reach out to us?

Thanks,

Your Trusty Sales Ace [Don't write this, though. Use your actual name!]

FORM SCREENING

Alternatively, you can use an online form to ask a series of qualification questions before you schedule a call. Just steal some questions from your diagnosis document (which you'll create in the next chapter), throw them in a Google Form, and ask the prospect to fill in their answers. Once you receive their reply, you can determine if they are sales qualified.

It's a numbers game. If you do no filtering of leads and try to talk to as many people as you can, you will close more deals. However, there is a point of diminishing returns, and sometimes preventing overwhelm outweighs the need to close every deal you can. Asking a quick question or two in an email will scare away fewer prospects than a ten-question discovery form will. Review your needs and filter appropriately.

ARE YOU ON THE LIST? LEAD SCORING FOR THE WIN

Lead scoring is a way to rank prospects to determine how each lead should be handled. If you're not already doing so, to make the best use of your sales resources, you should implement some amount of lead scoring. It does not have to be complicated or exotic.

The main benefit of good lead scoring is that it increases sales efficiency and effectiveness. It can help you determine if a prospect is qualified to talk to a salesperson, if they should stay in the marketing follow-up bucket, or if they should be referred to one of your Magic Wheel partners for some free cash.

Beyond basic filtering, lead scoring can drive increased sales and revenue by helping you focus your best resources on your best leads. If you have a high-scoring, high-value SQL, you might give it to your top rep. If you have a lower-scoring lead, you might pass it to a less-experienced ace in training. Also, lead scores help you prioritize your pipeline and determine the level of effort you apply to the diagnosis, sales engineering, and presentation processes. Lower-scoring leads get less effort and attention than higher-scoring ones.

Lead scoring can help your organization align marketing with sales by establishing standard definitions and benchmarks for what makes good lead. The marketing team can refine their strategy and targeting by using the lead characteristics identified by the sales team as the best indicators of success.

Last, lead scores for deals you've won can be used during

the transition to your delivery and account management teams to communicate a new client's potential churn risk. This will give your account managers and subject matter experts a better sense of how to handle the first few months of an engagement and increase the chances of creating the foundation of a long-term relationship.

Although a full treatment on lead scoring is beyond the scope of this book, here are a few tips to get you started.

Lead scoring models use specific prospect data points just like your ideal client profile such as:

1. Company size
2. Job title
3. Industry segment
4. Geographic location
5. Their stated budget or service request
6. Their email domain (@gmail.com versus a professional company domain)

Certain scoring models use behavioral data such as:

1. Number of times the prospect has visited your website
2. How many marketing emails the prospect has opened
3. Whether they downloaded a specific content offer from your website
4. Link clicks in emails or visits to specific pages on your website

There are a variety of methodologies ranging from quick eyeball tests to formal point-based systems tracked automatically by your CRM. Find something that works for you and use it to improve your focus, effectiveness, and efficiency.

Okay, you've attracted leads and dazzled them with your speedy response. It's time to start the diagnostic process.

KEY TAKEAWAYS FROM CHAPTER 5

- Speed sells. Responding to leads quickly can make or break sales success.

- Once you get a prospect on the phone, slow down. Take the time to understand their situation and needs before you start selling.

- If necessary, implement prescreening procedures to avoid wasting time with tire kickers.

- Implement lead scoring to help you prioritize the best opportunities.

CHAPTER 6

DIAGNOSE ROOT CAUSES

"A wise man can learn more from a foolish question than a fool can learn from a wise answer."

—BRUCE LEE

This chapter is one of the most important in the book. After executing a diagnosis call, I've had many prospects say, "This sounds great, Forrest. I'm looking forward to working with you." These reactions come before I've even done a formal sales presentation.

A diagnosis call (also known as a discovery call) is the first time you speak with a prospect to discuss their needs. You are probably already doing discovery calls in some form. However, if you're like 90 percent of the clients I work with, your diagnosis process is too rushed, missing critical questions, and not well documented. When your approach is incomplete and inconsistent, you're losing deals you could be winning and making it harder to train new sales staff.

Before we dig deeper, it's important to understand the steps and goals of the diagnosis call so you know what we're trying to accomplish. There are eight:

1. Build rapport
2. Explain the process
3. Prequalify
4. Discover needs and diagnose problems
5. Fully qualify
6. Strategize to energize
7. Answer pressing questions
8. Close the next step in the process

In addition to understanding the steps and goals, you have to have the right mindset.

MINDSET SHIFT: FROM ORDER TAKER TO SALES DOCTOR

People go to the doctor because something hurts. They want the doctor to figure out what's causing the pain and prescribe a treatment that will provide relief.

Most prospects come to you in the same situation. They have "pain" in their marketing function and they hope you can fix it.

Have you ever had a prospect say something like, "Hi. I own a footwear company, our organic rankings have been slipping, and we need link building to get them back up. How much does your link building cost?" Many prospects show up believing they have properly diagnosed their situation and have prescribed the right solution. They just want you to "take their order."

Now, if you went to your doctor and said, "My temperature is 103°. Please prescribe some amoxicillin," the doctor would laugh at you. The doctor prescribes the solution, not the patient. Good doctors are not order takers; they are strategic consultants.

In many cases, self-diagnosing prospects are wrong or only partially right. Whether you have a prospect playing doctor or one who sees you as the expert, remember that ace salespeople are not order takers but strategic sales doctors.

ACE IN THE HOLE

Like people seeing a doctor, you are reading this book because you have sales "pain" and you hope this book will help you relieve it. The same problem/solution dynamic is at work when people take my online courses or hire my consulting company. And it's the same reason your prospects contact you. Be a digital marketing doctor, not an order taker.

In chapter 3, I taught you a process for diagnosing your lead generation problems and mentioned that the diagnosis process can be used with your prospects, too. The diagnosis call is when you put on your white lab coat and grab your stethoscope.

So what does a good doctor do before she prescribes a solution?

She understands the symptoms and diagnoses the problem.

How?

By asking questions.

Not random questions. Specific, predetermined questions designed to uncover the patient's symptoms and problems. As a doctor moves through their diagnostic questions, they carefully record the patient's answers for future reference.

In the simplest terms, here is a doctor's process:

1. Ask questions to understand symptoms.
2. Use basic diagnostic tools (such as a thermometer) to begin to zero in on the problem.
3. Either through naked-eye observation or use of more-advanced diagnostic tools (such as X-rays), identify the root cause(s) of the problem.
4. Based on the information collected and years of experience, prescribe the right treatment.

Using the Clone the Ace system, you're going to do the same thing. Your prospects are in pain and they hope your services are the solution. By asking good questions and taking a real interest in their business, you build rapport and trust.

First, you ask questions designed to understand the *symptoms* your prospect is experiencing in their business, specifically with their marketing. Second, you use basic diagnostic tools (questions and/or quick online analysis tools) to pinpoint the *problems*.

In the next chapter, we're going to go into more detail about the sales engineering process I recommend. This is your advanced diagnostic tool to help you nail down the *root causes* of the prospect's problems and prescribe the right *strategic solutions*.

We're about to go through the structure and flow of the call and the exact questions you should have in your diagnosis template.

But before you get on the call, you need to prepare.

HOW TO PREPARE FOR DIAGNOSIS CALLS

What research should you do prior to the first call? How long should you spend preparing? What information should you prepare? There are no hard-and-fast rules, but there are some important guidelines.

When I first took over sales at my agency, I was inexperienced and terrified. I was still young enough to care way too much about what people thought of me and did not want to sound stupid. So what did I do? I would spend one or two hours before just about EVERY discovery call making sure I was super ready. Dumb. Necessary, I guess, at my stage of development, but dumb, and a mistake *you* should avoid. Here's why.

Obviously, you don't want to come off as unprepared, but you don't want to waste time either. Just because someone wants to discuss hiring your agency does not mean they are a good fit. How many times have you gotten on the phone with a prospect only to realize three minutes into the call that their budget is too small or they want a service you don't offer? If you spend an hour doing research on an unqualified prospect, you lose an hour of your life that you'll never get back.

Although prospects with very high lead scores may warrant more pre-call research, my default setting is to spend about five to ten minutes preparing. What I've learned over the years is that most prospects do not expect a full-blown proposal on the first call. My mindset is, "I don't really know how serious this prospect is or what they need. So let me just hop on the phone and see what's up."

See what's up. That's all I need to do. If after the first few minutes they seem qualified, the diagnostic questions you'll ask are the research. You don't do a lot of research before the call; you do it on the call, after you've determined it's worth your time. If you really know your services, you can handle most situations on the fly.

Now, I don't want to sound like an unprepared dumbass on these calls, so I'll of course review whatever information the client provided in their initial contact. Then I'll spend five minutes poking around their website and MAYBE their LinkedIn profile to get a high-level understanding of their business and their background.

If you're nervous or new to sales and doing a bit more research helps you feel confident, go for it. Just don't overdo it or believe hours of research are required for sales success.

CONDUCTING THE DIAGNOSIS CALL

I almost never do first discovery meetings in person. I definitely never drive to a prospect's office. If their office is nearby and they want to waste their time driving in to see me, fine. They can do that. Otherwise, my mindset is basically the same as it is for doing limited research: I don't know you, you don't know me, so let's just hop on a call and see if we have a ball game before we start wasting time driving across town.

If you're doing marketing nationally, this is less of an issue in that most of the people you speak with don't work anywhere near your office and don't expect an in-person meeting. Even if a huge, seemingly awesome prospect contacts me, I start with a call to make sure there is real potential. I've closed many large deals with well-known brands (including Amazon, Overstock, and Costco) 100 percent over the phone without even using video.

Let's get into the nitty-gritty details of the diagnosis questions and process.

THE FIRST FIVE TO TEN MINUTES OF THE CALL: BUILD RAPPORT, EXPLAIN THE PROCESS, AND PREQUALIFY

Okay, your agency is in the pole position. You've attracted a lead, responded quickly, and prepped for the call. Grab your microphone. It's finally time to get on stage and start selling those sweet solutions you offer.

Merriam-Webster defines rapport as "a friendly, harmonious relationship; a relationship characterized by agreement, mutual understanding, or empathy that makes communication possible or easy."

How do you build rapport? In two simple steps.

ASSUME RAPPORT

When I get on a call, my mindset, before anyone even utters a word, is that we're already good friends. And what's easier than talking to a good friend? There is no pretense. You don't have to watch what you say. It's the opposite of being on a formal job interview. We don't want our discovery calls (or any of our sales calls) to feel stiff, strained, or robotic.

BE REGULAR OLD YOU

If you assume you and the prospect are already friends, you can just relax and use the same tone you use when you walk into a coffee shop and see your best buddy. Yes, of course you should maintain a basic level of professionalism and not start cursing like a frat bro, but get your energy up, put a smile on your face (even if the prospect is not in the room with you), and start off with something simple and non-businessy. A question. A comment about something going on in the world that day or week (not political, please).

The key here is to just be yourself. Don't twist yourself into some formal salesperson pretzel. Even if the prospect on the other end of a phone is the CEO of a HUGE company, they're still a regular person who wears shorts and flip-flops on Saturday, farts, and drools on their pillow when they sleep, just like you. Treat them respectfully, but don't put them on a pedestal.

"Hey, Sherry. Where ya calling in from today?"

That's how I start almost every diagnosis call. It's a simple, friendly question unrelated to digital marketing. And it's an easy way to start a "normal" conversation and begin to build rapport. If their answer reminds me of a trip I took to their city or family I have who live in their state, I'll mention that. I'm just trying to find a connection point or get a quick laugh. Use whatever basic opener works for you.

ACE IN THE HOLE

If you're not comfortable asking a simple question and then building rapport on the fly, you can do a few minutes of research on LinkedIn or the prospect's website bio and find something to build an opener around. For example, if a prospect's profile mentions they love fishing, you can start the call with something like, "Hey, Jim, I noticed on your LinkedIn profile you're way into fly fishing. Have you taken any trips lately?" The point is to find something unrelated to business to kick off the call in a personal way.

If done well, I can actually hear a subtle sigh of relief on the other end of the phone because this person now feels like they are talking to a friend. They realize they are not talking to a slimeball salesperson who's trying to steal their kid's college fund. They start to open up and become more receptive to what I have to say. Remember, this is authentic. It's not a trick. It's just you being human. Being yourself. And that's refreshing and comforting in a world of automated phone trees, chatbots, and robotic telemarketers reading from scripts.

A bit of small talk is good, but don't overdo it. You don't need to talk about the weather for ten minutes. After a minute or two of friendly banter, begin the formal discovery process, but keep it friendly. It's formal only in the sense that you have specific questions you need answered, not in terms of the tone of the call. A good way to make the transition from friendly banter to the business end of the call is to lay out your sales process. You can say something like the following. Adjust to your own style.

> Sherry, on this call I want to better understand what you need help with to see if we're a good fit for each other. I have a bunch of questions about your situation, and then of course I'm happy to answer your questions. If this call goes well and we both think it makes sense to take the next step, I'll have our experts do an audit of X [whatever they contacted you about] and then we'll set up a time to go over the insights and opportunities we uncover as well as the formal scope of work and pricing. Sound good?

If they say yes and do not raise any red flags, they are pre-qualified to spend another twenty to thirty minutes with you. Move into the questions that follow.

THE MIDDLE TWENTY MINUTES OF THE CALL: UNDERSTAND THE PAIN AND FULLY QUALIFY

In the first five minutes, you got up on stage and said, "How ya doin', Detroit?" The crowd roared. Rapport was built. It's time to rock and roll. The next twenty minutes are some of the most important of the entire sales process. You'll employ the two most powerful tools sales pros use to build trust and set up the close: probing questions and active listening.

Diagnosis questions fall into four buckets. Familiarize

yourself with all the question types and adjust them to your circumstances.

My good friend and fellow sales ace Jay Mays contributed to this section of the book. Besides adding in some of his favorite discovery questions, here are a few of his "pro tips." They will help you use the questions more effectively.

- "Ask, don't sell" is always the rule during the first conversation. Although building rapport and trust is technically part of selling yourself and the agency, we are not yet presenting solutions and trying to close the deal. The diagnosis call is about getting the prospect to open up and setting up the close, which will happen at the end of the formal presentation.
- The best questions are open ended and allow the prospect to elaborate and unload.
- Diagnostic questions need to sound natural and conversational. It's not an interrogation.
- Diagnostic conversations never happen in a specific order. You flex and flow in a conversational manner.
- Diagnosis is never completed in a single meeting. It's a roadmap that guides all your future conversations. Diagnosis is also never done. Where sales leaves off, the account management and delivery team continues to discover client needs and the ways in which they can delight them over the course of the entire relationship.
- The easiest and most natural way to start a conversation is with challenges.
- Remember, authenticity rules.
- Like a great reporter, always follow your curiosity.

Okay, now let's cover the specific diagnosis questions, why

we ask each one, and what sort of information each one should pull out of the prospect.

General Business and Problem Questions

With the first set of questions, you're just trying to get the prospect talking about what's going on. Right after I'm done with the rapport building and laying out the sales process, I'll usually ask a question like the following:

> "I see from your form submission that you contacted us about building a new website and doing some Facebook advertising. Why don't you give me a quick overview of your situation and a bit more detail about what you need help with?"

This question should get them talking about the symptoms and pain they are experiencing. Listen carefully for key words and phrases that indicate something particularly important to them. Jot those down.

Jay's version:

> "What has changed in your business to make this a priority right now?"

Jay's version of the question gets you to their real why. If they don't know why they contacted you, it's either not a real problem or they were directed by their boss to "go get three quotes" and you're not talking to the main decision maker.

As they open up, feel free to ask follow-up questions to dig into their symptoms and problems. If they mention something that sounds important or interesting to you but you need more detail or clarification, dig deeper. "You mentioned X. Can you clarify why that's important to you?"

Besides listening intently and taking good notes, you should also have your qualification hat on. They qualified to have an initial call and prequalified to continue the call, but do they qualify to receive a full proposal? If you hear any red flags during the middle section of the call, don't be afraid to stop, confirm what you're hearing with follow-up questions, and even cut the call short if it's clear they are not a fit.

For example, if a prospect alludes to a really small budget and I know my services are not cheap, I might stop and ask a follow-up question such as, "Sorry to interrupt, Sherry. You mentioned your budget is pretty small. Our services are fairly priced, but they are not cheap. I just wanted to check in to make sure we don't spend time going down the wrong path. What sort of budget do you have?"

Alternatively, if you don't want to ask directly what their budget is or they say they don't know what it is, you can throw out your typical fee range and ask if it's a fit (more on budget questions later in this chapter).

If you're not hearing red flags and their situation seems like a possible fit, ask a few more probing business questions, such as the ones below, to fully flesh out their perceived problems and needs. You don't have to ask all of them. Pick the ones relevant to your situation and include them in your diagnosis call template.

What do you think is the right solution?

This question may have already been answered in their opening response. If not, it's an important one to ask directly, as it helps you see if they are self-diagnosing or truly looking to you as the expert. If they have self-diagnosed and done it correctly, you're going to parrot back what they said and match them throughout the sales process. If they are wrong, partially wrong, or say they have no idea, you're going to steer them to the right solution through research and education.

What is your business model and pricing strategy?

The answer to this question helps you uncover business issues they may not be aware of, further qualify the prospect, and begin to figure out a possible marketing strategy. Are they a manufacturer selling unique products or a drop shipper selling generic products that can be found cheaper on Amazon and fifty other websites? Are they generating leads for their sales team or selling leads to third parties, as HomeAdvisor.com does for contractors? The prospect's answer to this question may tell a story about broader problems beyond the specific marketing services they are looking to purchase. It may also help you confirm that you have a Winnable Game on your hands.

What marketing tactics are you currently using to drive traffic to your site?

This question can help uncover additional opportunities. Maybe they called about content marketing and they mention that they manage paid search in-house. If you offer paid search services, you can ask if they want help with that, too. Also, if they contacted you about paid search services and, when you ask this question, you realize they are not using a complementary service such as A/B testing for their landing pages, you have an opening to present a more comprehensive solution that will produce better results (or refer them to a Magic Wheel partner). These are just examples. Adjust to your situation.

What is your unique value proposition? Why should people buy from you?

Again, you are probing for potential business issues or positive attributes that help you understand how likely you are to be successful. If they are reselling generic brown boxes with no differentiation, it might not be the right deal for you. As we discussed in the positioning chapter, there are times when you can improve a prospect's marketing campaigns and still not have a positive impact on their bottom line because they have fundamental business issues that can't be fixed by doing better marketing.

What are your specific, measurable goals? Jay's version: How will you measure the success of this solution?

Like the good sales doctor you are, if you can help them, you are eventually going to prescribe a treatment plan. And whatever you ultimately propose, it needs to be a solution that gets them from where they are (in pain) to where they want to go (feeling good about their marketing results). The first few questions were designed to understand their current state. This question identifies their desired future state, which is important not only to figure out the right strategic solutions but also to make sure their expectations are reasonable and represent a Winnable Game for your team.

What is your budget for these services?

Although we don't want to ask this question in the first five minutes, we don't want to wait until the end either. Before I learned this lesson, I had many great forty-minute discovery conversations only to find out near the end that the prospect didn't have the budget to hire our agency.

I've gotten to a point in my career where I don't have any problem just straight up asking what their budget is. Jay has another way to address the budget issue that might work for you if you're hesitant to ask directly.

How did you come up with a budget for this solution?

Jay's version is a more indirect way to broach the budget topic. If they say they don't have a budget, you can talk about your minimum fees or throw out a range by saying something like, "Our social media services typically range from $3,500 to $5,000 a month. Does that sound like it's within your budget?"

Regardless of how you ask about their budget, approach it sooner rather than later. You can cultivate your confidence around this issue by reminding yourself that there is nothing to be nervous about. They know what you do costs money. The sooner you both address it, the sooner you know if you should keep talking or not, and that's good for both parties.

Nervousness typically comes from being attached to closing the sale. Remember that EVERYONE wins some and loses some. Drop your attachment to closing every deal and ask the budget question.

> ### ACE IN THE HOLE
>
> Whenever you throw out a price range, the prospect expects (or at least wants) your proposal to come back at the bottom of the range. Either make your range smaller or just make sure the bottom number is pretty close to what you think your proposal will be. Once a fee estimate escapes your lips, they will hold you to it. If you're unsure and don't want to box yourself in by hastily throwing out a price (or even a range), you can buy some time by telling the prospect you have to check with the team and you'll get back to them right after the call.

Logistical Questions

Next, you'll want to dig into their technology, relevant digital assets, and current baseline statistics so you can determine if they are a good fit. For example, if someone is calling for help with their WordPress site and you don't work on WordPress sites, you need to know that before you start putting a proposal together.

Ultimately, you need to ask the questions that make sense for the services you offer. If you sell copywriting services, it may make no difference what technology their website is built on or what analytics package they use. But if you are talking to them about SEO services, those things matter greatly. Here are some additional examples:

- How often do you post to Instagram (or send emails, write blog posts, etc.)?

- What are you using for analytics?
- I see you use Mailchimp; how is that platform working for you?
- How many users or visits does your website average each month?
- How many leads or sales do you get each month?
- What is your average order value per customer and/or the lifetime value of a customer?
- What are your current results from X? (For example, if they called because they are not happy with their site's conversion rate from paid search, dig into what their current rate is and how they track it.)
- Any other qualifying questions you need to ask to determine if the services you are discussing are a good fit for your agency's approach and the client's stated goals.

At this point, you should be able to determine if they are fully qualified to work with you and where the conversation needs to go next. If they have become unqualified, tell them why and ask if they'd like a referral so you can grab some Magic Wheel cash. If they are qualified, move on to the rest of the diagnosis questions.

Resource Questions

It may be important for you to understand which resources (besides budget) the prospect is bringing to the table and which they expect you to provide.

For example, my agency offered conversion rate optimization services but did not offer any design or development services. Our clients had to implement our recommendations themselves. As such, to make sure our approach was going to work for them, it was critical to ask questions about the prospect's development resources up front.

As in the last section, you need to ask the questions that are most relevant to the services you offer. Which questions you should ask in any part of the discovery call ultimately depends on what information you need to diagnose the problems, fully qualify the prospect, and begin to sketch out a solution. Here are some example resource questions you can use.

Do you have internal resources for X, or are you looking to us?

X could be anything relevant to the services you're discussing: developers, designers, copywriters, and so forth. Again, this will help you further qualify and begin to develop ideas on scope of work and pricing. If they need you to set up and manage their display advertising, it might be one price. But if they need you to do the graphic design for the ads, too, it might be a different price.

How many people are on your marketing team?

This question helps you understand the size and sophistication of the prospect's organization. Depending on your ideal client profile, their answer to this question may make them more or less qualified.

If we end up working together, who would be our main point of contact?

This question will help you get the lay of the land, figure

out how you might structure the formal presentation, and determine the role in the buying process of the person with whom you're speaking.

What is your level of expertise with the service(s) we're discussing?

This question is critical in that it clues you in to how you should communicate with this person and how you should present your solutions to them. If they know little to nothing about the service they are interested in, you need to stay away from industry jargon or complex concepts so you don't speak over their head. If they are very technical or highly experienced in internet marketing, you might need to have some of your top subject matter experts on the presentation call to talk shop, impress them, and make them feel warm and fuzzy.

Buying Process Questions

This last set of questions helps you understand their approach to purchasing your services. Asking these questions will help you end the discovery call well and, even more importantly, tailor your post-discovery call process to resonate with how they are behaving as a buyer. Here are some key questions you should ask.

Who else are you talking to?

Although we don't necessarily need to know the names of any other agencies the prospect might be considering, it is important to have a sense of the situation. When a prospect says, "I have a list of fifteen agencies I'm contacting," it's a less appealing opportunity than if they say something like, "I'm just speaking with you guys and one other agency, but I really think you guys might be the right option." Depending on their answer, we may make them a higher or lower priority. We'll discuss this further in the next section.

> In finding an agency to help with X, what's most important to you? Also, is there anything you are looking to avoid from past bad experiences?

"When people realize they're being listened to, they tell you things."

—RICHARD FORD

This is my favorite question and one of my guilty pleasures in selling. When you ask these two related questions and get some good, specific answers, it's basically like the prospect whispering in your ear, "Here is exactly what you should say to win my business."

The more times you ask (and then shut up and listen), the more they'll tell you. When they stop talking, don't be afraid to say, "Is there anything else?" And then do it again. And again. Until they have emptied all the info out of their brain and into your notes.

If they say something like, "Well, my last agency took two weeks to get back to me every time I emailed them. That drove me nuts. I want an agency that is responsive," well, guess what slide is going to be in the proposal deck: one about how we're proactive and responsive and have an internal policy that requires all employees to reply to clients within twenty-four hours during regular business days.

During the formal sales presentation, we are going to parrot back the information they provide using the exact words and phrases they used. This works like magic to make them feel like they were listened to (which they were) and that we're on the same wavelength (which we are).

The reason I call it magic is not that we're being inauthentic; it's that it's common for the formal presentation to happen two to seven days after the diagnosis call. During the time gap, the prospect will forget what they said to you. So when you parrot back their top needs and concerns using the exact wording they used, it subconsciously feels like you are reading their mind and builds warm, fuzzy trust.

The way I just presented this makes it sound a little slimy. But if you do it with the right intention, it's not. All you are doing is asking what they really, really want for Christmas. If you come from a place of authentically wanting to help them, there is nothing sleazy about asking someone what they want, listening intently, and then giving it to them. In fact, it's a rare gift that you can give a prospect to win their trust and their business.

> What is your time frame for making a decision and getting started? Jay's variation: What determines timelines on your end?

However you ask it, this question is designed to pull out

their internal timelines and priorities so you can match your solution to their situation. Just like when we ask what their success goals are, this question helps us make sure we set proper expectations. If they say they need a new website up in two weeks and you know it's going to take two months, you can discuss that now, reset their expectations, or if you can't meet their timeline and they're not willing to adjust it, not waste time putting a proposal together.

Who else is involved in the decision-making process?

If possible, we want to have all stakeholders and decision makers attend the formal presentation. If we can't get access to all the decision makers during the sales process, we can at least ask our contact what's important to each of them and make sure we address it in our proposal, which they're likely to review after the live presentation.

THE LAST FIVE TO TEN MINUTES: STRATEGIZE TO ENERGIZE, ANSWER QUESTIONS, AND CLOSE THE NEXT STEP

The first thing you want to do near the end of the call is to provide what I call a Strategic Solution Sketch. The discovery call is fundamentally about the first two parts of the diagnosis process: understanding symptoms and identifying problems. The sales engineering and presentation processes we will cover in chapters 6 and 7 are what you'll use to pinpoint the root causes of the prospect's problems and develop the full scope of your prescribed solution.

The Strategic Solution Sketch is not the full strategy. It is, as the name implies, a preliminary prescription, similar to a doctor saying, "Well, we are going to have to wait for the results of the MRI, but based on what I'm feeling, I think you're going to need arthroscopic surgery on your MCL. Let's get you scheduled for that MRI."

When you do a little light strategic consulting on the discovery call, you immediately increase your credibility and go from sales slime to trusted partner. You are giving them hope that they have finally found someone with a brain who can help them hit their marketing goals. If you do this well, especially when your Strategic Solution Sketch is different from what the prospect self-diagnosed, you'll strengthen their belief that you are the best option.

If you have solid knowledge about your services (which you must) and you've taken the time to ask good discovery questions, you should find yourself in one of these four scenarios.

They're Right

The client's self-prescribed solution (the service they called about) turns out to be the exact right solution to their problem. In this case, you simply confirm what they suggested. "Based on what you've told me, I agree with you that link building is the right solution here."

They're Wrong

The client's self-prescribed solution was totally wrong. For example, after asking your diagnosis questions, you realize that although the prospect contacted you to launch ads on Facebook, the nature of their business indicates that they would do better with Google Ads. When a prospect is wrong, you need to explain why and then recommend that they shift their focus to whatever strategy you believe will be more effective.

They're Partly Right

If a prospect contacts you because they want to increase organic search rankings and they believe better link building is the solution, but you believe that they must fix some critical technical issues on their website before link building will work well, the prospect's diagnosis is only partially correct. In that case, you need to explain why link building is not the entire solution and why they need to consider a broader approach that includes technical SEO.

ACE IN THE HOLE

Sometimes you'll find that the service the prospect wants is strategically accurate but is not a complete solution and your agency does not offer the complementary service they need to hit their goals. In that case, be generous and authentic. Tell them what other services they need and why. Then offer to make a referral to one of your Magic Wheel partners.

You're Not Sure

Last, you may come across prospects you think you can help, but for one reason or another, you are not 100 percent sure what to recommend. In this case, just be honest. You might say something like, "Based on our conversation, I'm pretty sure we can help you, but because you were not able to tell me the details of X, Y, and Z, I need to check with our social media team before I let you know for sure that we're a good fit and what the best solution would be."

This is no different than when a prospect asks you any question you don't know the answer to. You don't make up the answer. You just say, "I don't know, but I'll ask the team and get back to you." The point is to always be honest and authentic. Always.

Answer Their Questions

After you present the Strategic Solution Sketch, you need to make sure most of their questions are answered. If you take my advice and make the discovery call structured but conversational, there is a good chance you'll get some questions from the prospect as you go. Whether they asked a bunch of questions or none, near the end of the call, you want to give them a chance to ask any lingering ones.

I started off the last paragraph saying you need to answer *most* of their questions. Why not all of their questions? As you'll see in the next chapter, sometimes people ask very specific questions for which you have a great slide in the pitch deck, and if you try to provide an answer without the visual aid or the broader context the presentation provides, your response won't have the same impact.

The bottom line is to answer what's pressing—the questions they *need* answered before they'll move on to the next step—but that's it. Take your time, make them feel heard, but stay in control of the conversation and the sales process. I will cover a few examples related to this concept at the end of this chapter.

Close the Next Step

Remember that throughout the entire process you always need to be *selling* and *closing* the next step. When you first emailed a lead to set up the diagnosis call, you told them what was going to happen on the call so that it seemed like a valuable use of their time. Do the same thing here. You're selling the value of the next step to get them to agree to move forward. In this case, the next steps are to allow your team to conduct research and create a formal presentation to recommend your solutions in person or via web conference. The presentation close should go something like this:

> "Sherry, after speaking with you, I'm confident we can help you. The services you need are right in our wheelhouse. What I'd like to do is have our paid search team take a look at your Google Ads and Facebook accounts. We'll create a formal presentation and deliver that to you via web conference in about three days. During the presentation, we'll share all of the insights and opportunities the team found, the scope of work, and of course the final price for our management services. Even if you don't end up hiring us, I can assure you the presentation will be educational and you'll get a lot of value out of it. Does that sound good to you?"

Assuming they say yes, you then wrap up by explaining what you're going to do after you end the call. For example, you might need to request access to their Google Ads and Analytics accounts so your team can complete their sales engineering research. To maintain momentum, end the call by telling them what you're going to do and then do it as quickly as possible.

If you can, schedule the presentation meeting before you end the diagnosis call. This helps create momentum. If you need to confirm dates and times with your sales engineers before you book the next meeting, do that as soon as possible after you hang up.

A note on the structure, order, and timing I've recommended for your diagnosis calls: these are guidelines, not hard-and-fast rules. If you spend a bit longer building rapport, fine. If you give your Strategic Solution Sketch ten minutes in or sprinkle it in along the way as opposed to all at the end, fine.

We just covered a lot of powerful diagnosis tactics. Even if you're a freelancer or a small agency with simple services, think twice before skipping any of them. That said, you're never going to be (nor should you be) an exact clone of me or any other agency. You are human and every prospect is a bit different. Implement what speaks to you, give things a try, and stay flexible. Refine your process as you go.

HANDLING COMMON QUESTIONS DURING DIAGNOSIS CALLS

Below, I cover common questions you'll probably get when you implement the diagnosis process I just covered.

TELL ME ABOUT YOUR AGENCY. WHAT DO YOU GUYS DO?

This question may come up at the beginning or at any time throughout the call. Essentially, you need an elevator pitch so you can cover the highlights of your agency's offerings and convey your unique value without getting into a full-blown sales pitch. Here is an elevator pitch framework you can use to build an effective response.

1. The first sentence should be your core positioning statement. It should let people know what you are and what's unique about you as an agency (or freelancer).
2. The one or two sentences in the middle should clarify your unique value.
3. Last, state as clearly and specifically as you can, what you offer.

Example:

> We are a boutique digital marketing agency that helps manufacturers drive sales through e-commerce stores. Not only do we specialize in working with manufacturers, but we also focus only on digital advertising. We don't build websites or claim to do fifteen different things. We're experts in a few specific tactics for a specific type of customer. We set up and manage paid online advertising on Google Ads, Bing Ads, Facebook, and Amazon.

Be flexible and natural with this. Yours can be a bit shorter or longer than the example. Just make sure it has all the elements I listed. And don't deliver it like you are reading a script. Get comfortable with it and deliver it like you would if you were at a coffee shop with a friend and they asked you what your agency does. Also, if you use networking as one of your lead attraction tactics, you now have a good answer when people ask you what you do.

WHAT ARE YOUR FEES?

Prospects may ask about your fees in their initial contact. If you have set packages, let them know the pricing levels. If you do custom pricing, let them know your minimums or typical ranges for the services they are asking about.

If a prospect asks about your fees in their opening email, it typically indicates that they have a smaller budget. In which case, telling them your fees and scaring them off sooner rather than later is an efficient move. If they respond and confirm your suspicion, don't forget to email them back and offer to refer them to a Magic Wheel partner.

If the fee question comes up on the diagnosis call itself, you're basically going to answer the same way. Straight-forward, clear, and confident. This is not a book on psychology, but please do what you need to get confident about stating your prices.

If you've done the work to become a good digital marketer and your team can produce good results, you need to state your pricing loud and proud. It is what it is. It's either a fit or not, and the best way forward is directly and authentically. So state your packages, minimums, and/or price ranges, and ask if they're within the prospect's budget. If they say yes, proceed. If not, refer them out and collect your free cash.

HOW MANY PEOPLE WORK AT YOUR AGENCY?

The reason I listed this question is not that it's a real hot one. But it's an example of the kind of logistical questions you may get—questions such as, "How many years have you been in business?"; "Where are your offices located?"; etc. The strategy here is straightforward. Give answers to about two to four logistical questions and then let them know you will cover all of their questions during the formal presentation.

As I mentioned earlier, you limit logistical questions on the first call because you will have great slides covering logistics in the presentation deck. Also, you can't let the prospect take over the call and shortchange the time you need to get through your critical diagnostic questions. You are the lead singer. It's your stage and your microphone. They can talk into it, but they can't hold it.

DO YOU HAVE ANY EXPERIENCE/CLIENTS IN MY INDUSTRY?

Most people ask this question because they regard prior experience with companies similar to theirs as evidence that you are qualified to help them. This question is tricky because no matter which way you answer it, the prospect may not be happy.

If you tell a prospect that you don't have any industry-specific experience, they may be disappointed and not believe you can help them. If you do have relevant experience, they might be kind of happy at first, but then they may resent it if they get concerned about confidentiality. Further, prospects may worry that you are going to learn on their dime and then use your knowledge to help their competitors.

Although it can go either way, more often than not, prospects see industry-specific experience as a positive. If they ask how you protect confidentiality between clients, just explain your policy. If you don't have a policy for this situation, make one. If you position yourself narrowly within a specific industry, this issue is going to come up more and more as you grow. There are several ways to take care of it, such as taking only a certain number of clients in each city or offering an exclusive engagement in exchange for a higher fee.

SERVICE-SPECIFIC QUESTIONS

Similar to logistical questions about your agency, these are nitty-gritty questions like, "How many blog posts do you write each month when you're doing content marketing for clients?" Again, answer two to four of them and let the prospect know they'll get all of these sorts of questions answered in detail during the formal presentation. Calm them down and keep the call moving.

If done correctly, at this point, the prospect may be pretty excited to move forward with you. At the very least, you'll have a fully qualified prospect who has a solid level of trust and is genuinely interested in seeing the insights and opportunities your team uncovers during sales engineering.

Next, we're going to go deep into the process of identifying root causes of the prospect's marketing problems and nailing down the full strategic solution you're going to propose.

KEY TAKEAWAYS FROM CHAPTER 6

- Conducting a good diagnosis call is one of the most important parts of the sales process.

- Don't be an order taker. Don't assume your prospects know what they need. Be a sales doctor who uncovers root causes before prescribing solutions.

- Diagnose prospect problems by asking the right questions and listening closely for prospects' key concerns and desires.

- Prepare for diagnosis calls, but don't overdo it. You usually don't know how good an opportunity is until you get on the first call.

- Before you talk business, build rapport and set the agenda for your whole process.

- Create a diagnosis call template that has all the questions you need to ask to thoroughly assess the situation, including questions about budget.

- Answer their questions, handle objections, and then sell and close the next step in your process.

CHAPTER 7

PRESCRIBE STRATEGIC SOLUTIONS

"Strategy without tactics is the slowest route to victory. Tactics without strategy is the noise before defeat."

—SUN TZU

I'm a total golf nut. If I did not have to make money to feed my son, I'd probably play every day. Since I do have to work, I try to play about twice per week. For most of my adult years, I rented a golf cart every time I played. Riding in a cart takes less effort and is more relaxing. I always rationalized riding over walking because I exercise at the gym five times per week.

As I got older, I started thinking about changing my workouts from the high-impact, get-ripped routines I learned when I was nineteen to lower-impact exercise such as swimming, walking, and stretching. I kept thinking I should walk more rounds of golf, but I was not ready to make the extra effort.

One day, it dawned on me that if I started walking the course, I could kill not just two but four birds with one stone. Let me explain.

I usually spend about an hour at the gym. About thirty minutes of my workout is spent doing something aerobic and high impact, such as running on the treadmill. Playing eighteen holes of golf takes about four to five hours and renting a riding cart is about $16 each time you play. If I make one simple shift, from riding to walking, here are the benefits:

1. I skip the high-impact aerobics at the gym, helping to preserve my joints.
2. I gain back 2.5 hours a week (30 minutes x 5 times a week doing aerobics at the gym).
3. I double or triple my exercise by adding five to ten hours a week of low-impact exercise without adding any additional time to my schedule.
4. I save about $120 in cart rental fees per month.

Implementing the sales engineering process I'm about to teach you is like walking when playing golf. It's a simple shift that provides multiple benefits at once. If you don't currently do much or any sales engineering, it may seem like conducting research would add a lot more work to your process. In reality, sales engineering can dramatically improve not only the efficiency and effectiveness of your sales efforts but also your entire operation and the profitability of your agency. Let me show you how.

KILLING EIGHT BIRDS WITH ONE STONE

First, let's define what I mean by sales engineering. Sales engineering, in the context of selling digital marketing services, is simply the process of having a subject matter expert audit and analyze information related to the services you're going to pitch.

So if you're pitching Facebook and Instagram advertising, you're going to have one of your experts (i.e., the people who actually manage Facebook and Instagram for your clients) look at their current campaigns and dig up insights and opportunities to improve results.

Let's return to the analogy of a doctor diagnosing a patient. When a patient visits a doctor and says they slammed their arm in a car door, the doctor might assume their arm is broken. But until they take an X-ray, they can't be certain. Sales engineering is your X-ray machine. It pinpoints root causes, confirms your suspicions, and provides additional context you can use to prescribe strategically sound solutions.

Here are the specific reasons to add sales engineering to your process (or to invest in improving your approach if you're already doing some research).

TAKE PRESSURE OFF YOUR SALESPEOPLE

If you use subject matter experts to help research, scope, and pitch your services, that's one less thing your salespeople need to do, which provides two direct benefits. It saves your salespeople time so they can be on more sales calls, and it dramatically reduces the pressure on your hiring process. You don't have to find someone who can sell AND knows all of your services at an expert level. That's two giant birds we just killed.

> **ACE IN THE HOLE**
>
> Using subject matter experts to conduct sales engineering research helps your sales process run more efficiently. By eliminating the need to hire salespeople with deep technical expertise, you make it easier to find competent professionals and allow those professionals to spend more time on sales calls.

IDENTIFY WINNABLE GAMES

The fewer prospects you let in who are going to cause trouble because you can't really help them, the fewer headaches you'll have. Clients who are not happy because they are not getting great results drain a tremendous amount of time, energy, and profitability from your agency. Sales engineering can prevent this from happening because your subject matter experts have the best vantage point from which to determine whether a prospect represents a Winnable Game or not.

SET YOURSELF UP FOR SUCCESS

Rather than being an order taker and simply selling the prospect whatever they called for, the sales engineering process transforms you into a sales doctor who creates and presents comprehensive strategies that can actually solve prospects' problems.

SET PROPER EXPECTATIONS

Creating a sound strategy and determining a scope of work based on actual research allows you to set proper pricing and client expectations. This prevents you from being in constant firefighting mode.

That's at least three more birds we just killed.

BUILD TRUST

As I'll discuss later in the book, many prospects have been burned by other agencies who overpromised and underdelivered. They're skeptical. Whether they have a bad taste in their mouth or not, some prospects have no experience with the services you are proposing and may be uncertain whether spending money on digital marketing will actually work for their business.

In either situation, being generous with your time up front and letting people know that you conduct the sales engineering process as much for them as for yourself (because you want to make sure you can help) builds trust. And trust, like confidence, closes deals.

IMPRESS PROSPECTS

As I said earlier, you're not really selling a service. You're selling your subject matter experts' experience in using the marketing tactics you offer to produce the bottom-line business results your prospect craves. If your marketers' expertise is the real product, having them on the call allows the prospect to get a taste of what they are considering buying. Assuming you have good people with great experience, by showcasing them on the call, you can further differentiate yourself from other agencies.

> **ACE IN THE HOLE**
>
> The experience of your subject matter experts (and the results they can produce) is your product. Assuming you have great people, injecting them into your sales process so prospects can get a real taste of what they're buying is a powerful way to differentiate yourself from other agencies and win more deals.

GET HIGHER FEES

Below is an unsolicited email from a prospect who ultimately became a long-term, multiservice client. He had just gone through our sales process while simultaneously getting pitches from three other agencies.

Mark   2:05 PM ☆ ↰ ⋮
to me ▾

Forrest,

Cards face up. We are very interested. You were at the bottom of our list because your initial monthly pricing was higher than the other firms we have spoken with. No one else has, however, taken the time to understand our brand, our products, and our customers as you have in this short time.

A rough count shows that we've killed eight birds with one move. Pretty powerful.

Okay, now you know what sales engineering is and why it's important for winning deals. Let's cover the basics of how to do it. In the next chapter, we'll demonstrate exactly what your research findings should look like in the presentation deck.

SALES ENGINEERING GOALS, DELIVERABLES, AND MINDSET

The sales engineering process has three main goals:

1. Determine if you can help the prospect achieve their marketing and business goals. Do they represent a Winnable Game?
2. Determine the appropriate strategy, scope of work, and pricing so you can set reasonable expectations, improve client retention, and maintain your profitability.
3. Convince prospects that you are the best option to help them achieve their goals by showcasing your team's expertise.

When conducting sales engineering, subject matter experts should look for insights and opportunities that help your team and the prospect understand the marketing challenges on a deeper level. For example, let's say a prospect contacts you because the return on ad spend (ROAS) from their Google Ads is too low. If you find that their campaigns are not using negative keywords and are wasting money on irrelevant search terms, that provides a deeper understanding of why their ROAS is so low.

Insights naturally flow into opportunities. In the Google Ads example, the insight that the prospect's campaigns are not using negative keywords indicates that there is an opportunity to improve ROAS by eliminating wasted ad spend and that hiring your agency may be a good investment. Also, insights drive scope of work. In this case, you should pitch the prospect a program that includes negative keyword analysis, implementation, and ongoing optimization.

A sales conversation in which you show specific insights and explain why they represent good opportunities to drive results is much more effective than one in which you say, "I see from your contact form submission that you're interested in paid search services. Great, we offer paid search management. Our fee is $2,500. Sign here." That's what order takers sound like. Sales engineering enables you to be a strategic sales doctor.

HOW TO FOCUS YOUR RESEARCH AND PRESENT INSIGHTS AND OPPORTUNITIES

For each service they pitch, sales engineers need to provide insights that *help* the salesperson prove that your agency is uniquely qualified to take advantage of the corresponding opportunities and improve the prospect's results.

When selecting insights, sales engineers should have the mindset that they need to deliver "surprising education." Whenever possible, we want to present at least some insights that prospects will not hear about from the other agencies they're considering.

The ultimate goal is to have the prospect hear about the insights and opportunities and make statements like the following:

1. Wow, I learned something new that I believe will improve my marketing.
2. Nobody else told me that.
3. Your agency is clearly different and better. I can see how you would improve my results.
4. Based on what you found, I should pick you over the other options I'm considering.

The sales engineers' research and insights should *support* the ultimate goal but do not need to be so amazingly in-depth that they sell your services all by themselves. Although critical, they are only one part of the presentation.

As you will learn in the next chapter, you're going to be presenting your insights using a slide deck. Each sales engineering slide will generally be a screenshot of some element of the prospect's marketing campaigns (like a screenshot of a Google Analytics report showing a problem) with a few bullet points or key words that prompt the sales engineer to tell the story of the insight.

Each insight is like a small story in the larger story (i.e., that you are the best option to help them use digital marketing to achieve their business goals). The formula for insight stories is as follows:

1. The prospect's stated problem.
2. A tactic-specific insight that is at least one part of the stated problem.
3. A brief explanation of what the insight means and why it's important.
4. An opportunity statement to connect your solution to the stated problem and client goals.

Here is an example of the formula in action.

Prospect's Stated Problem

My conversion rate used to be 2.5 percent, but after a recent website redesign, it's slipped to 1.75 percent. I want to get the conversion rate back to where it was.

Tactic-Specific Insight that Is at Least One Part of the Stated Problem

Analysis of your Google Analytics account shows that after the redesign of your website last year, the conversion rate on your desktop site remained relatively flat, but the conversion rate on your mobile site dropped by 30 percent. Furthermore, the number of visitors using site search on mobile dropped by 62 percent.

Additional analysis shows that your old mobile site offered a prominent search bar that was pinned to the top of every page on the site, whereas your new mobile site has search hidden behind a small magnifying glass icon making it much less prominent.

Explanation of What the Insight Means and Why It's Important

These insights are critical because your analytics show that mobile visitors who use site search are ten times more likely to convert than those who do not use site search.

Opportunity Statement to Connect Solution Back to Stated Problem and Goals

By conducting further analysis and applying best practices, we can recommend specific ways to change your website that will get mobile site search usage back up to (and above) previous levels. This is one important step in getting your site-wide conversion rate back to 2.5 percent.

It's fine to "give away" a couple of prescribed solutions. However, you want to focus mostly on presenting the problems and root causes. Don't give away so much that they say, "Great, let me go fix all those things you just showed me and I'll get back to you if we need more help."

In our conversion example, we could mention the insight about the difference in mobile conversion rates but leave out the part about how their old site had a persistent search bar. Excluding specifics about the solution would cause the prospect to wonder what's different about the two mobile sites and be eager to work with you if they believe you have the answer. The point is to give them a *sample* of a tasty cookie to get them hungry for more. If they want the whole box, they need to pay you.

A powerful way to present specific solutions while still driving the prospect's desire to hire you is to say something like, "We found ten specific insights and opportunities you can use to increase your conversion rate. Let me show you two of them now." If the two insights and solutions you show are impressive, they'll practically beg you to let them hire you so they can know about the other eight opportunities.

APPLY THE APPROPRIATE LEVEL OF EFFORT

If you don't typically do any sales engineering, obviously I'm asking you to spend more time than you do now. On the other end of the spectrum, I've had clients hire me as a coach or consultant because they were spending too much time on sales engineering. Just how much time should you spend? What's too much?

The general rule is that you should spend just enough time to accomplish the goals of sales engineering without going overboard.

I recommend having five to ten standard insights you can look for in each service area. If you sell paid search advertising, for instance, pick several areas of an account you always look at, such as an account's use of match type, negative keywords, and other campaign settings that tend to cause problems.

Standardize your list and build it into your presentation template (I'll show you how in the next chapter). Refine as you go. If prospects consistently seem underwhelmed, you may need to add more or better insights. If they are wowed but you're spending eight hours on each presentation, you need to dial it back.

> ### ACE IN THE HOLE
>
> Create a standard list of research topics by service area and build slide templates for each one. Pick topics based on how well prospects respond to them in sales presentations and refine your list over time. In the end, you will have a way to quickly uncover persuasive insights and build them into your presentation deck without having to reinvent the wheel each time.

Although large sophisticated sales opportunities may require more time, you should generally spend around thirty to ninety minutes on each service area or tactic you are going to propose. If you are going to be auditing multiple services, each one should have its own bucket of research time.

If you spend close to two hours in any one research area and feel like you need even more time, stop and determine if more time is really necessary. What questions have you not answered? What few things are critical to wrap up so that you achieve the goals of sales engineering? Over time, your team can refine your process by asking the following questions:

1. What sort of insights do clients always seem to like? Make those insights more robust and/or standard.
2. Which insights often confuse people or generate little positive response? Can we improve them, or should we delete them?

3. Are there any areas that are connected to the popular insights that we should add in to complete the story? For example, if people like that you typically do insights on match types for paid search but you don't really talk specifically about negative keywords, which is related to match types, you might add a slide about negative keywords and link the two concepts together to tell a complete tale.

In terms of the number and scope of your insights, there are two guidelines I recommend you follow.

The first guideline is, within reason, to cover the entire service area. List all the parts of a service and have insights for each. For example, if you offer comprehensive SEO services, you want to have some technical SEO insights, some content insights both for foundational content and strategic content, and some link-building insights.

The second guideline is to have one to three insights for each part you need to cover. If you have a very hot opportunity with a sophisticated client, you might have a few more insights than if you're pitching to a small company with limited digital marketing experience. A ballpark number would be five to ten individual insights for each service you're presenting. That may or may not translate into five to ten slides. You might have two or three insights on a related topic on one slide.

If you're spending what you think is a reasonable and profitable amount of time and delivering insights that are consistently wowing prospects, you're in the sweet spot. If not, adjust as necessary. Remember that templates and checklists are your friends here. Have a list of standard stuff to investigate. Don't reinvent the wheel every time you open up a prospect's Facebook account to conduct research.

A NOTE ON NONEXISTENT CAMPAIGNS

How do you do sales engineering on marketing tactics that are brand new for the prospect? If someone calls about launching an Instagram influencer campaign and they don't even have an Instagram account for their business, obviously you can't audit what does not exist.

When there is nothing of the prospect's to audit, you can use examples of what their competitors are doing, best practices, and case studies. You can also do some general research and offer a mock-up of your solution sketch. The point is that you should still provide educational insights and opportunities that indicate hiring you is a good investment.

Now that you've conducted your research, you need to turn it into a world-class presentation that will seal the deal. The techniques and templates I cover in the next chapter will help you create each presentation quickly and easily.

KEY TAKEAWAYS FROM CHAPTER 7

- Use subject matter experts to uncover prospect-specific insights and opportunities that will help you develop the right strategy, scope of work, and pricing.

- Although sales engineering can seem like you are adding a lot of work, it can save you a ton of time in the end. When done correctly, sales engineering will help you win more deals and ensure that you're bringing on clients who represent Winnable Games. This increases client retention and employee satisfaction.

- Sales engineers should strive to provide "surprising education," revealing things that the prospect was not aware of and that other agencies are not pointing out.

- Train your sales engineers to find and develop insights that make it clear your services will take advantage of the opportunities you found and result in the client achieving their bottom-line business goals.

- Create standard lists of common research areas to save time, and refine your lists as you go to ensure you're delivering insights that have a powerful impact on the prospect.

CHAPTER 8

HOW TO CREATE PRESENTATIONS THAT WOW AND WIN

"People don't remember what we think is important. They remember what they think is important."

—JOHN MAXWELL

A couple of years ago, I had a company come to my home to discuss replacing my windows. It was one of the best sales presentations I've ever seen but not because the salesperson was so amazing. Don't get me wrong, the rep was well spoken, professional, and seemed sincere. However, what really stood out was the mechanics and flow of the pitch.

The sales rep was at my house for two to three hours and went through a meticulously choreographed presentation. I felt like I was watching a ballet. He used finely tuned discovery questions and relevant talking points to begin the conversation. Next, he presented slides on his laptop that were professionally designed, engaging, and made some powerful points (pun intended).

Toward the end of the pitch, he pulled out props, including a sample of his company's window along with those of a few of his competitors. He aimed a high-powered heat lamp at the competitor's window and showed me the temperature reading on the other side. He then asked me to extend my hand to feel the heat coming through the window and then did the same with his company's product. There was a massive difference in the amount of heat getting through each window.

If saving energy and reducing drafts in my home were important, his windows were obviously the best choice. He did not just tell me his products were better; he *showed* me with a tangible experience of the difference.

When it came time to try to close, he had several very specific techniques and talking points that were pretty powerful. He was dogged in his approach without being pushy or slimy. Every part of the presentation flowed right into the next in a logical sequence, and there were many times when he called back to earlier parts of the pitch and connected the dots. It was super impressive.

Here's the kicker. He did not create the presentation. He did not develop the sequence, the questions, the example slides, or the idea to use the window props. He had literally nothing to do with the creation of the pitch. A true sales ace had developed the presentation and installed it in his company so all the sales reps could copy it.

The window company used a blueprint to build a powerful presentation that anyone with basic sales skills and a little practice could deliver with great results. They cloned the ace. I estimate that the design of the presentation represented 80 percent of its effectiveness. The salesperson's delivery accounted for the other 20 percent.

Below is an unsolicited email from a prospect I pitched digital services:

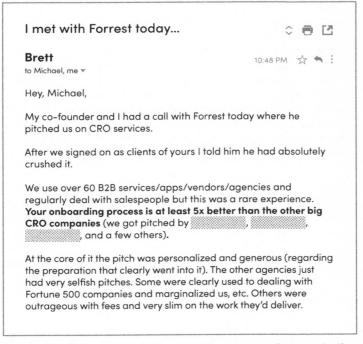

I met with Forrest today...

Brett   10:48 PM
to Michael, me ▾

Hey, Michael,

My co-founder and I had a call with Forrest today where he pitched us on CRO services.

After we signed on as clients of yours I told him he had absolutely crushed it.

We use over 60 B2B services/apps/vendors/agencies and regularly deal with salespeople but this was a rare experience. **Your onboarding process is at least 5x better than the other big CRO companies** (we got pitched by ▓▓▓▓▓▓▓▓, ▓▓▓▓▓▓▓▓, ▓▓▓▓▓▓▓▓, and a few others).

At the core of it the pitch was personalized and generous (regarding the preparation that clearly went into it). The other agencies just had very selfish pitches. Some were clearly used to dealing with Fortune 500 companies and marginalized us, etc. Others were outrageous with fees and very slim on the work they'd deliver.

Unsolicited email from a prospect who received the same type of presentation I'm teaching you.

The sentiment in the above email is one I've heard after many of my presentations. I've also seen my clients build out their own version of my pitch deck and get similar reactions.

This chapter is going to teach you the exact structure I used to produce the result shown in the email above. You can clone my presentation, just like the window company did with theirs. You'll be 80 percent of the way to ace level without even improving your sales skills. In the next chapter, I will teach you how to deliver the presentation so you get positive responses on a consistent basis.

ACE IN THE HOLE

In the email testimonial about my presentation, the prospect said that one of the things he liked was that "preparation... clearly went into it." Although the sales engineering of course took some time, the presentation format is based on a template, so it took me only fifteen minutes to customize a few slides. To the prospect, it seemed like I'd spent several hours, which I did, but only the first time when I created the original template. That's the power of templates.

WARNING: DO NOT DO THIS, UNLESS YOU WANT TO LOSE DEALS

In chapter 3, I coached you to never just email proposals to prospects. You must first present them live. Let's explore why this is so important.

If your current sales process is to do a discovery call and then email a generic proposal thirty minutes later and you do win some deals, you may object to the recommendation that you spend a lot more time putting together a custom presentation and delivering it live. There are three reasons why you need to shift your thinking and implement what I'm going to teach you in this chapter.

YOU'RE LOSING DEALS

Although emailing a generic proposal after a brief conversation can work, it's not optimal. You may win some deals, but you're definitely losing others that you could be winning. Why? You're doing what many other agencies do, which makes your agency look like a generic brown package. You're missing an opportunity to differentiate yourself.

Also, if all you do is email a dry proposal and standard agreement, the prospect has nothing with which to compare you to your competitors but a list of tasks, some legal mumbo jumbo, and a price. Not super compelling.

YOU'RE LOSING MONEY

Emailing generic proposals after a quick discovery call may be fine if you're selling $500-a-month cookie-cutter programs to small businesses. But if you're trying to sell (or you'd like to be selling) $5,000-a-month SEO programs to larger, more sophisticated organizations, a generic email proposal is not going to cut it.

YOU'RE ACQUIRING CRAPPY CLIENTS

A friend of mine owns a paid search agency that caters to companies with teeny tiny budgets, and he does well. That's pretty rare. His business model requires meticulous checklists and low-wage contractors to remain profitable. Generally, the smaller the client, the bigger the headaches. Unsophisticated clients tend to have unrealistic expectations, lots of anxiety around spending money on marketing, and as a result, need more hand-holding along the way.

When your sales process is so quick and easy, because all you have to do is change the name and date on a generic proposal and shoot out an email, you're likely to send it to almost anyone who contacts you. If, however, you take the time to audit their accounts, develop a real strategy, and create a customized presentation that has to be delivered live, you're going to think twice about whether someone is qualified to work with you.

Even if you target smaller clients with fixed packages and simple needs, you're still going to have better success with a live presentation of your proposal AFTER you've done a discovery call and customized your presentation template to the prospect's situation.

POINT OF CLARIFICATION: PRESENTATIONS VERSUS PROPOSALS VERSUS AGREEMENTS

I talk with a lot of agency owners and salespeople, and I'm never quite sure we're speaking the same language when it comes to the difference between a presentation, a proposal, and an agreement. I don't really care what you call these things, but I want to define and distinguish these terms so you have a clear understanding of what I mean by each one. Whether you use my terms or your own, make them standard and share them with your team so everyone is on the same page.

WHAT IS A PROPOSAL?

A proposal is a detailed list or description of the work you're recommending the client hire you to do. Proposals include information such as the price of your services and estimated delivery dates. When agencies email out a basic proposal, the "proposal" document often includes the agreement. Despite typically being contained in the same document, proposals and agreements are two different things.

WHAT IS AN AGREEMENT?

An agreement is a legally binding contract. Although agreements usually contain and incorporate the proposed scope of work, they also cover the legal terms and conditions that govern the relationship between your agency and the client.

WHAT IS A PRESENTATION?

In my system, a presentation is a slide deck that contains a variety of educational information about your agency, the insights and opportunities you gathered during sales engineering, and your proposal. The presentation is both a document (the slide deck) and an action you take (presenting it) to convince a prospect you're the best option. As discussed in the previous section, only after you present the deck do you send a copy via email.

The formal agreement, which contains a description of the work proposed in your presentation, is sent once the prospect says that they want to see an agreement or that they want to hire you. Don't waste time creating and sending out agreements until someone asks to see one or says they're ready to move forward. The presentation should close the deal, and the agreement, while obviously important, is mostly just paperwork to memorialize the client's decision.

HOW TO STRUCTURE YOUR PRESENTATIONS

The presentation structure I'm about to teach you has been developed and refined over seventeen years. It's battle tested, and when combined with the design principles I teach in this chapter and the delivery skills I'll teach you in the next chapter, prospects often say it was the best they've ever seen.

Although you can test, tweak, and modify the structure to fit your situation and style, you should, one way or the other, include all of the core elements we'll cover or have a very good reason for skipping any particular slide.

The basic structure of your presentations should be as follows:

1. Reestablish the rapport you had on the diagnosis call
2. Demonstrate what your agency offers and why it's different and better
3. Introduce specific services and why they are different and better
4. Cover the prospect-specific insights and opportunities your sales engineers have gathered
5. Show and explain return on investment calculations (i.e., value selling)
6. Review your proposal and pricing

7. Present case studies and supporting examples of your work

Now let's get specific. Below is a list of all the presentation components with explanations of what each slide is supposed to cover. In the sections that follow, I'll dig deeper into how to create and deliver each type of slide. There is a lot of information here. For now, just let it wash over you. When you're ready, go back through this chapter and follow the steps to create your own template.

LOGO SLIDE

The first slide in the deck should have your agency logo or other identifying information. This is nothing more than the "cover page" to identify the creator of the slide deck. If you want to include the date of the presentation, the prospect's name, or any other relevant information to help orient the viewer, that's fine. Just keep it simple.

ACE IN THE HOLE

One thing I like to do right at the start of a presentation, while the logo slide is still up on the screen, is to let the prospect know I'll be sending them the entire deck after the call. This lets them know they don't have to take copious notes. They are free to relax and just soak in the information. This puts them at ease and gets them more focused on the pitch.

CONTEXT/PARROT SLIDE

The next slide should include highlights of the diagnosis call. The purpose of this slide is to reestablish the rapport you built on the first call and show them that you were listening to their needs. The slide includes three to five bullet points that cover the topics the prospect said were important. When possible, parrot back the exact words and phrases they used.

SERVICE OVERVIEW

Even if you think the prospect already knows, create a slide that showcases all of the services your agency offers. There are several reasons this is important:

- If the prospect is considering several agencies, they may have forgotten your service mix since you last spoke. This slide will remind them which agency they are speaking with.
- There may be people on the presentation call who were not on the diagnosis call and don't know the background of your agency or what services you offer.
- Often, people will not be aware of all of your services, and covering your entire menu can lead to upsells. Although you should try to uncover upsell and cross-sell opportunities on the diagnosis call, sometimes things slip through the cracks. When I go over a general service slide during the presentation, it's common for prospects to say things such as "I did not know you guys offered social media. I'd like to talk to you about that, too."
- You'll be sending the presentation deck to the prospect after the call, and decision makers who were not on any of the previous calls may review it. Covering all of your services gives the new people important context about your agency.
- Finally, a service slide allows you to reiterate your ele-

vator pitch and easily segue into the next slide. Even if you have only one service, you may still want to have a slide that allows you to talk a bit about why you have that single focus and how it benefits the prospect.

AGENCY-LEVEL DIFFERENTIATORS

On this slide, you're going to cover your unique value at the agency level. You can put all of your differentiators on one slide, or you can make a slide for each differentiator. You should have at least two or three real, relevant differentiators. More than five is too many. Remember that these differentiators are about your agency as a whole. In other parts of the slide deck, you'll talk about the unique value you offer at the service level. Here are a few examples:

1. We specialize in patient acquisition for plastic surgery practices.
2. We build WordPress websites in one week.
3. Each client gets a team of three people working on their account. Many other agencies assign only one person.
4. We have proprietary software that produces 30 percent more sales from social media.

THIRD-PARTY PROOF

If you have any awards, impressive partnerships, or other third-party credibility that helps substantiate your claims of superiority, create a slide showcasing that information.

If you are a newer agency or otherwise don't have much third-party credibility to show, you can use client testimonials or case studies. Over time, build real proof of your proficiency as a practitioner of the services you offer and add it to your presentation template.

Anytime you can include impressive logos from well-known, reputable organizations you're associated with, put them in your deck. Examples include BBB A+ logos, industry association logos, awards, and so forth.

FACTS ABOUT YOUR AGENCY

This slide answers common questions such as where your offices are located, how many employees you have, how many years you have been in business, and so on.

Do your best to highlight relevant things, even if they are from your last job or some other agency you worked at. For example, if your agency is new but you worked on fifteen accounts and produced great results when you were at another agency, you can still talk about that experience. Just be up front about the situation.

Whether you choose to include an agency facts slide or not, be prepared to answer questions about background, years of experience, and other logistical matters, as prospects will ask them.

CLIENT LOGO SLIDE

Another way to differentiate and build trust is to feature the logos of clients you've worked with in the past. Well-known brands are always nice to feature.

If you don't have any/many impressive logos to feature, you

can skip this slide for now and build it out as you acquire clients. When possible, tailor the logos to the prospect's industry.

SERVICE OVERVIEW SLIDES

Each service you are pitching should have one or two overview slides. Service overview slides allow you to talk about how you deliver that particular service and the unique value you offer at the service level, as opposed to what differentiates your agency as a whole.

For example, one of your agency-level differentiators may be the industry within which you specialize. When it comes to a specific service, such as content marketing, you might have a unique way of creating and promoting content, or an award you won for that particular service.

INSIGHTS AND OPPORTUNITIES FROM SALES ENGINEERING

This is the meat and potatoes of the presentation and highlights the insights and opportunities you uncovered during the sales engineering process.

The length of this section is dictated by the nature of the service(s) you audited and how valuable you scored the lead. For example, if you have a prospect considering you for management of their Google Ads account, you might create one to three slides for each key part of the account. Search, remarketing, display, and shopping would each have one to three insight slides. If you audited their SEO, too, you'd have a separate section of slides with the insights you uncovered about that service area.

ROI CALCULATIONS OR ESTIMATED RESULTS + TIME FRAME

Although it was always a good idea, given how many prospects have been burned by other agencies, discussing projected revenue results has become pretty much mandatory. It's great to show your differentiators, clearly point out the opportunities the client has, and make a proposal for how to take advantage of them. But eventually, prospects are likely to ask you what results they can expect and by when.

Since I can't cover the methods for calculating potential return on investment (ROI) for every type of digital marketing service, I recommend that you find what works best for the services you sell. However you do it, make sure you present numbers that set proper expectations and help the prospect justify the investment.

Note that you don't always have to present exact revenue numbers. You can discuss averages and probabilities, too. For example, a slide showing that your services give the prospect a 70 percent chance of increasing traffic by 30 percent within six months may be sufficient.

If you're selling to a prospect with a ton of low-hanging fruit and you know for certain you can crush it, let them know. If, on the other hand, you come across a situation in which you believe you can be successful, but there are some unique challenges that make predicting results a bit more difficult, don't be afraid to mention the challenges and set appropriate expectations. Here is an example:

> "Chris, we've seen this issue before, and we are reasonably confident we can help resolve it. That said, we need to let you know up front that since X, Y, and Z are unknown, we can't give you a firm timeline of when you may see improvement."

Whether good or bad, call it like you see it. Honest assessments will increase your credibility and save you from the pain that inevitably comes when you overpromise and underdeliver.

Here are four additional benefits of building an ROI section into your presentation, courtesy of my friend Jay Mays:

1. Quantifying value demonstrates critical thinking and builds credibility, which further evolves your sales professionals from order takers to strategic consultants.
2. Quantifying the value of your proposal helps your sales team have authentic conversations about your pricing and short-circuits price-based objections. If you're claiming (and can back up) that you can produce $10 for every $1 a prospect spends with you, price becomes a phantom objection.
3. Showing a strong, bottom-line business case can help you close deals during a downturn in the economy, such as the one caused by the 2020 coronavirus pandemic.

4. Providing ROI calculations empowers your prospect to have internal conversations with CFOs and other financially focused members of the decision-making committee.

PROPOSAL WITH PRICING

The proposal usually takes up one to three slides explaining exactly what you're recommending the prospect purchase from you. Proposal slides should cover the scope and pricing of your work, including the specific tasks, deliverables, time frames, and things such as meeting and reporting frequency. Be sure to include enough detail to proactively answer common questions prospects have about what they will get for their money.

If you sell only one service or sell all of your services as one package, you may have one set of proposal slides at the end. If your agency sells services à la carte, you might have multiple proposals in the same pitch deck. For example, you may have one or two proposal slides for building a website, one for SEO services, and one for paid search management at the end of each service section in your deck.

Ultimately, the content from your proposal slides will be copied over to the formal agreement, so make them as detailed as they need to be without getting too deep into the legal terms and conditions of your contract.

CASE STUDIES, EXAMPLES, TESTIMONIALS, AND AWARDS

You should have these elements on your website, but it's a

good idea to have two or three case studies and/or examples of the exact work you're pitching in the deck. They can go at the end of each service section, in an appendix, or wherever they fit best.

You don't necessarily have to cover these slides during the presentation, but it's a good idea to have a few in your template because prospects often request case studies and references. During the actual presentation, you can mention the case study slides and let them know they can review the details when you email them the deck.

If you have any service-specific testimonials or awards you've not already covered at the beginning, you can place them at the end of each service section.

NEXT-STEPS SLIDE

You can end with a slide that prompts you to transition into discussing the next steps in your sales process. We'll cover exactly what to say at the end of the presentation to close the deal in chapter 10.

REFINE YOUR DECK OVER TIME

Internet marketing is constantly evolving, and you should treat your presentation deck as a living, breathing document. You can add slides to cover new concepts. You can change the order to improve the flow. You can swap out case studies as you grow and remove slides that don't seem to resonate with your prospects.

Keep a log of common questions. If you hear the same

question over and over again, that's an indication your deck is missing a slide. Over time, you'll begin to anticipate what information your prospects want, and you can proactively address common areas of interest by adding new slides.

HOW TO BUILD AND DESIGN YOUR PRESENTATION FOR MAXIMUM IMPACT AND EFFICIENCY

If you're thinking that this all sounds like a lot of work, you're right. It is. But, as I mentioned earlier, it's only a lot of work the first time you make the standard slides.

You're not going to build a deck from scratch every time. You're going to build a template that takes the salesperson about ten to thirty minutes to customize for each presentation (not including sales engineering research). Not only will your template be flexible and efficient, but the design tips I'm going to show you will make it visually and intellectually dazzling, too.

HOW TO BUILD A QUICKLY CUSTOMIZABLE PRESENTATION TEMPLATE

Approximately 70 percent of your slide deck will be made of standard slides that rarely ever change, which I call static slides. These include the following:

1. Logo/Cover
2. Agency Service Overview
3. Agency-Level Differentiators
4. Third-Party Proof
5. Facts about Your Agency

6. Client Logos
7. Service Overview Slides
8. Case Studies and Work Examples
9. Next Steps

You should take the time, using the design tips covered in the rest of this chapter, to make these standard slides as professional and compelling as you can. You don't need to be a graphic designer to make them look great. I'll show you some quick shortcuts. However, if you don't have any design skills or otherwise can't make them look professional, hire a freelancer to jazz them up for you. Professional design makes a big difference, and you can get it done inexpensively on sites like Fiverr.com or Upwork.com.

A NOTE ON PRESENTATION TEMPLATES

Although the slide types I listed above are basically static, that does not mean they are set in stone. For the most part, these slides will not change from pitch to pitch. However, feel free to make one-time, prospect-specific changes or general improvements over time. If a standard slide includes something a particular prospect will not like or is missing something they will want to see, make a change for that one pitch.

If you have a new, more compelling case study you'd like to include, by all means replace an older one. If you create your cover slide in a way that requires you to insert the date and the name of the prospect, of course you'll update those elements each time.

Exceptions aside, the standard slides should be pretty

much exactly the same over the course of about a year or two. At which point, you may want to do a substantive refresh or complete redesign to reflect changes in the industry and the evolution of your agency.

The other 30 percent of the deck will be slides that are partly static and partly customized for each pitch. Customized slides and sections include the following.

THE CONTEXT SLIDE

Create a format for this slide and then just fill in the specific bullet points based on your diagnosis call notes.

THE INSIGHTS AND OPPORTUNITIES SLIDES

These are the slides the sales engineers insert during their audit process. Create blank slides in each service section that have titles prompting the sales engineers to research specific parts of client marketing campaigns and assets.

These slides should be designed to help the sales engineers deliver insights that tell a complete, logical story. More on how to build these slides in the next few sections.

THE PROPOSAL SLIDE(S)

These are the "prescription" slides with the specific scope of work and pricing you're recommending based on your research. If you sell set packages, you can make standard, static slides that outline what's included for each service package you offer.

Even if you are selling custom solutions, you can usually create a large majority of the proposal slides as templates and just customize the price and a few other specifics. For example, if you sell SEO services that are customized for each client, you probably do many of the same tasks for most clients. In that case, you can standardize the descriptions of common tasks so you're not starting with a blank slide each time.

ACE IN THE HOLE

If you sell multiple services or have multiple options for each service, include slides in your template for every service and package you offer. This way, when you make a copy of the template for the next prospect you're going to pitch to, you can simply delete any services or slides that are not relevant to that particular pitch.

ACE IN THE HOLE

Although some slides, like the sales engineering ones, will be mostly customized, you can standardize certain parts. For example, if you always research match types when pitching Google Ads management, you can have a standard match type explainer slide that's always in the deck. Also, although screenshots of a prospect's paid search account will be specific to their account, they can be screenshots of the same type of reports for every prospect.

CREATE COMPELLING, EDUCATIONAL STORIES

The deck format and structure I've laid out in this chapter form a story that follows this basic flow:

1. This is what we heard from you on the diagnosis call.
2. This is who we are.
3. This is why we are different and better.
4. This research shows why and how we can help you achieve your goals.
5. This is exactly what we'll do to get you great results.
6. Here is how much it will cost and your expected return on investment.
7. Here is proof from third parties that we can do what we claim.
8. By now, it should be clear we are the best choice.
9. Here is how you take the next step.

That is the overall story. But as you build your customized slides, you need to be telling substories within the larger story. For example, you can't just have a slide that says you're better because you have excellent customer service. Everyone says that. Plus, every prospect expects good service as a basic requirement. However, if you have a slide that helps you tell a more detailed story, like the following one, it's way more impactful.

> Over the years, prospects have told us they get super frustrated by agencies that take a week to answer emails. They expect the agency to be more responsive to their needs.
>
> To make sure we provide excellent customer service, we have implemented three specific procedures:
>
> - All employees are required to respond to client emails and voice mails within twenty-four hours during regular business days. To keep this rule top of mind, it's posted on the wall in our conference room.

- All clients have a minimum of two people on their account plus the department director. This ensures that even if people are on vacation, there is always at least one person available who is familiar with your account.
- We send an automated email message to every employee at 3:30 p.m. every day to remind them to respond to any outstanding client requests.

The above example shows how you can promise customer service in a way that's about eight billion times more effective than just saying "we have great customer service." Further, when you marry your stories with compelling visuals, as I'll show you how to do in a minute, you're going to win more deals. Period.

MAKE SURE YOUR STORY MATCHES REALITY

Your sales presentation is the story of your agency. If you don't have a good story to tell, you may have to change your agency. For example, if you want to tell a story about a twenty-four-hour customer response policy, and you don't have a twenty-four-hour response policy, you need to create one. In other words, prospect desires drive changes not only in the messages you deliver in your sales presentations but also in the operations of your agency.

Your product (i.e., your services and how you deliver them) and your sales presentation are not two disconnected things. What you say should match what you do. Your sales story should come from a combination of the needs and desires of the market as well as your natural strengths as an agency or freelancer. If your story stinks, change your agency. Create new products. Hire better employees.

Do what you need to do to *really* be the best option for your ideal clients.

MAKE IT VISUAL AND ENGAGING

"If you think presentations cannot enchant people, then you have never seen a really good one."

—GUY KAWASAKI

Everyone hates slides with lots of text and bullet points. Everyone knows everyone hates those slides. Yet, many people still make slides with tons of text and bullets. Please stop.

Although certain slides may need to have a bunch of text (like your detailed proposal slides or slides with sales engineering insights requiring explanation), most times, a picture, a couple of icons, or just one word is enough to prompt you to tell a story in a far more engaging and effective way.

Let me give you a specific example using the customer service story we just covered.

STANDARD SLIDE EXAMPLE

This common slide design often results in sales reps reading the text while the prospect dozes off, drools on their keyboard, and wants to die.

To make sure we provide excellent customer service, we have implemented three specific procedures:

1. All employees are required to respond to client emails and voice mails within twenty-four hours during regular business days. To keep this rule top of mind, it's posted on the wall in our conference room.

2. All clients have a minimum of two people on their account plus the department director. This ensures that even if people are on vacation, there is always at least one person available who is familiar with your account.

3. We send an automated email message to every employee at 3:30 p.m. every day to remind them to respond to any outstanding client requests.

VISUALLY ENGAGING AND MEMORABLE WAYS TO TELL THE SAME STORY

This next example uses professional-looking icons to *prompt* the sales rep to tell your engaging story of differentiation, rather than writing it out word for word and reading it like a robot.

The next example allows you to tell the same story using a large, attention-grabbing image.

This is one of my favorite deck-building tactics. It looks awesome and takes no real graphic design skills. I simply grab relevant pictures from Google Images, www.unsplash.com, or a paid stock photo site when copyright issues are a concern.

This approach works especially well when the image is in color. Not only does it act as a prompt for your story, but it also helps prospects anchor your message to a memorable visual.

This slide looks cool and is memorable. It took me thirty seconds to "design" by inserting a relevant image and typing the storytelling cues on top of it.

SALES ENGINEERING SLIDE EXAMPLES

Let's assume you're pitching conversion rate optimization services. Your deck template would have five to seven blank slides with a prompt on what sort of insight the sales engineer should include.

In the first example, we're asking the sales engineer to find a conversion rate optimization insight that relates to the home page of the prospect's website. If it's an e-commerce site, you then might have slides with prompts for a category page, a product page, and a step or two in the shopping cart. This format allows the sales rep and the sales engineer to tell a complete story about opportunities for improvement from the home page all the way through checkout.

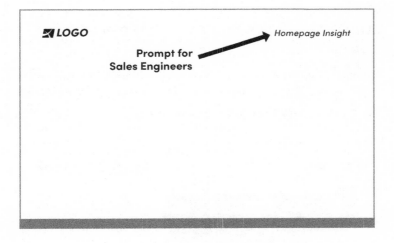

CRAPPY INSIGHT SLIDE

◪ LOGO   *Homepage Insight*

Your homepage is one of the first pages most visitors will land on. As such, it's very important to create an experience that is engaging and leads the visitor to the next step. On your homepage we noticed the following insights and opportunities.

1. Long-winded sentence that tries to point out something insightful but is too much text for the prospect to take in during your presentation.

2. Long-winded sentence that tries to point out something insightful but is too much text for the prospect to take in during your presentation.

3. Long-winded sentence that tries to point out something insightful but is too much text for the prospect to take in during your presentation.

SLIDE WITH VISUALS THAT ENGAGE AND PROVIDE CONTEXT

Instead of a ton of text, we have a screenshot of what we're talking about and short prompts to remind the sales engineer what story they are supposed to tell.

As I taught you in chapter 7, it's best to highlight a problem and allude to the solution rather than give detailed instructions for how to fix the issue. That said, when in doubt, err on the side of being generous with your insights. It helps prove you know what you're talking about and that your agency would be a good choice to help the prospect achieve their goals.

> **ACE IN THE HOLE**
>
> Use slide animation tools sparingly. If you have five points to make on a slide and you want to reveal each one after you finish the last to prevent people from reading ahead, that can be a good use of animation. Don't overdo animation by having elements fading, spinning, and flying around on more than a handful of slides.

HOW LONG SHOULD YOUR DECK AND PRESENTATIONS BE?

As short as possible but as long as necessary to tell the whole story.

If you use the visual techniques I've just taught you, cover interesting and valuable insights, and tell engaging stories about how you are going to make money for your prospect, they will be more than happy to sit through a sixty-minute presentation with fifty slides. If your deck is only fifteen slides, as long as you cover the important points and close deals, fine.

If you're presenting multiple services for a big, complicated engagement, it's rarely a good idea for the presentation to be over ninety minutes. If you need more time than that, set two presentation meetings so you have enough time to answer all of the prospect's questions without rushing. Visit www.clonetheace.com to download a sample presentation deck.

Just like it did for the window salesman I discussed at the beginning of this chapter, a great presentation template can handle about 80 percent of the work of convincing a prospect to hire you. Nevertheless, sales and presentation skills are still important, and that's what the next chapter is about.

KEY TAKEAWAYS FROM CHAPTER 8

- Build a presentation deck by following the structure and techniques in this chapter and you'll be 80 percent of the way to consistently getting great results.

- Do not email proposals to prospects after a quick first call. Customize your presentation template and present it live (in person or via web conference).

- Be sure to sell not only the scope of work you're proposing but also the value of your services by presenting return on investment (ROI) calculations.

- Build a quickly customizable template to create efficiency without sacrificing effectiveness.

- Your presentation deck should be designed to tell compelling, educational stories about how your services will achieve the prospect's business goals.

- Show, don't tell. Use visually appealing slides to prompt you to tell stories rather than reading text-heavy bullet points.

- Refine your slides over time to improve relevance, flow, and impact.

CHAPTER 9

PITCH PERFECT

HOW TO DELIVER YOUR PRESENTATIONS LIKE AN ACE

"The best way to sound like you know what you're talking about is to know what you're talking about."

—HARVEY MACKAY

The infinite monkey theorem states that a monkey hitting keys at random on a typewriter keyboard for an infinite amount of time will eventually write any given text, such as the complete works of William Shakespeare.

The premise of this book is that if you copy me, you'll get the same results I do. To this point, the book has been about helping you understand the framework and processes I use so you can follow in my footsteps.

That said, whether a monkey can write *Romeo and Juliet* by blindly banging on a keyboard or not, you can't produce great sales results by blindly copying a sales system. You still need to use your brain and develop sales skills that bring the system to life and allow you to write your own version of my story.

This chapter is about some of the specific sales skills and tactics I've developed over the years that will help you use the blueprint I'm presenting in a way that substantially improves your results. In chapter 12, we'll talk more about how to customize the entire system to your specific situation and skillset.

We're going to cover eight powerful sales skills. The skills presented are based on seventeen years of serious study and lots of in-the-trenches trial and error. Regardless of what you're selling or what sales system you're using, these eight skills can help you close more deals.

First, a note about how and where you'll be presenting. As I've mentioned several times, with rare exception, we never email prospects a presentation deck before presenting it live. Don't even send it a few minutes before the pitch. The first time they see your slides should be when you're presenting them.

One of the main reasons for this is that if you follow the design tips I just showed, you will create many slides that have only one big picture and a couple of words. As such, a good portion of your presentation deck will not make much sense to someone reviewing it without your eloquent stories and explanations.

To that end, we always present live in a professional office setting or via web sharing software. Although there is no right or wrong way, I personally like presenting via web conference with no video cameras on. Many people swear by presenting in person or at least using video so they can monitor body language and keep people focused.

For me, having only the slides and audio works best. Without video, there are fewer things to be distracted by or worried about. Does my shirt have a stain on it? What does it look like behind me? Is that a booger on their nose? Because I know my deck is visually appealing and the content super engaging, I don't want the prospect or me to be distracted by nonessential input.

This is personal. If you sell to lots of local clients and you want to do your pitches in person or you like having the camera on while you're pitching, knock yourself out. Just know that a screen share platform and a pitch deck is technically all you need. I've sold literally millions of dollars' worth of huge deals to some of the largest companies in the world without even seeing my counterparts' faces.

Let's get to the skills that pay the bills.

SALES SKILL #1: IDENTIFY BUYER TYPE

You don't talk to a five-year-old child the same way you speak to your forty-eight-year-old boss at work. Similarly, you should not speak to every prospect the same way. The first skill you should develop is the ability to quickly identify the type of person you're presenting to and cater your presentation to their learning style. This helps you build rapport and allows the prospect to easily process what you're telling them. You should try to do the identification during the diagnosis call. It affects not only how you present but also what you put in the pitch deck in the first place, so it's good to know as early as possible. (Note: when you deliver the presentation, you may have to quickly assess new people who were not on the diagnosis call.)

How do you do this? Two ways.

ASK AND LISTEN

First and most important, you ask good questions on the diagnosis call and listen intently. You'll not only gather facts about the person (e.g., their job title) but also pick up on what type of person they are. Do they speak quickly or slowly? Do they seem to be more keyed in on the numbers or the strategy? Are they analytical or more emotionally oriented? Do they seem well versed in the services you're discussing, or are they a newbie? Are they highly technical or more business-oriented?

MEMORIZE THESE BUYER TYPES

Second, familiarize yourself with the most common buyer types so you can sense their style more easily. Below are the buyer types you'll encounter on a regular basis.

Note that some prospects will represent several of these types. For example, you could speak to two different Chief Marketing Officers and one could be a highly technical, fast-talking know-it-all, whereas the other is strategic, not technically oriented, and has an open, soft communication style. Don't overthink or overdo this. You still have to be you. Just listen and then gently adjust for their style.

THE BURN VICTIM

The internet marketing industry has a real credibility problem these days. In just the last couple of years, I've spoken to over a thousand prospects looking to purchase digital marketing services. I estimate that 80 percent of them were unhappy with their last agency (or every agency they had ever hired). Unfortunately, regardless of their job title or speaking style, the burn victim is the type of person you're going to encounter most often.

There are a lot of snake oil salesmen in the digital marketing industry slinging subpar services and pissing people off. Because of this, many of the people you're going to be presenting to fundamentally will not trust you or your industry. They are clinging to the hope that yours will be the first agency to do right by them. But they will be skeptical until you loosen them up through a different sales experience than they are familiar with.

Whatever the prospect's previous agency did to piss them off is obviously not your fault. That said, you still need to acknowledge and address their negative experience. The best way to deal with burn victims is to ask them to explain exactly how the other agency disappointed them. The most common answers you'll get are:

1. They promised the moon but did not deliver.
2. The sales pitch was great, but then they put me with some kid fresh out of college who barely knew what they were doing.
3. It took them forever to respond to my emails.
4. I felt like I always had to come to them with campaign ideas and mention new developments in the online

marketing world. I was paying them to be the expert, but they were not proactive.

5. They were good people, but they just did not produce good results.

Dealing with burn victims is a perfect illustration of why positioning and building your agency is part and parcel of a successful sales function and why I say everyone is on the sales team. If you're going to successfully sell to burn victims (and keep them happy over the long term), you can't just say, "We don't do any of those things your other agency did." You actually have to be better. Like, for real. Then you can use a few slides and an authentic story or two to prove you actually are different and better.

Besides using sales engineering to show them why you're substantively better at digital marketing than their last agency (and the other agencies they are considering), you can't skip over their skepticism about the basic functioning of your agency, how you provide great customer service, and what you do to get the bottom-line business results other agencies couldn't deliver. You need to make it clear HOW it's going to be different this time. The customer service slide and story examples in the last chapter illustrate what I'm talking about here.

THE NEWBIE

The newbie lacks experience with the services you're discussing but not necessarily with marketing or business in general. They could be a great business leader or a super-sharp ten-year marketing veteran who simply has no experience with the specific marketing tactic you're discussing. The point is to find out their level of experience during the diagnosis call.

You'll learn plenty about their general level of knowledge just from their title and from hearing them talk about their situation. Asking a direct question such as "What is your experience with programmatic advertising?" will instantly tell you how high- or low level you need to speak.

Once you know their level of experience, you can adjust your presentation content (both the slides and what comes out of your mouth) accordingly. This advice applies to all buyer types. If you have a few people on the presentation call who were not on the diagnosis call, get a quick read on them by asking a question or two about their levels of experience and areas of interest. Use the style best suited to whom you believe is the key decision maker in the group and check in with the others as necessary.

THE INTERN

Although they might not literally be an intern, this buyer type represents a person who has little to no decision-making authority. They are typically younger and may be an admin or lower-level marketing person the boss directed to "go get three SEO quotes."

When you identify this buyer type, you should do whatever you can to encourage them to have the decision makers on the presentation call. Some sales pros would tell you to not waste your time with these people because if they can't get direct access to the decision maker, they kill the deal. I don't follow that philosophy. If I tried to get the decision maker on the call but can't, and the prospect is otherwise well qualified, I don't have a problem pitching to the intern.

If you refuse to pitch because a particular decision maker won't get on the presentation call, you will 100 percent lose the deal. Plus, the approach to presenting I'm teaching you can wow an intern even more easily than a grizzled veteran. By presenting to the intern, you may end up with a really excited internal champion promoting you to their boss as the best of the bunch. Ultimately, to pitch an intern or not is a personal decision based on factors such as how good of an opportunity the prospect represents, how badly you need the business, and so on.

If you pitch an intern, you're going to do all the same things you do for any other prospect plus pay attention to the fact that they want to look good to their boss. When the owner of a company is your audience, they care mostly about getting results. The intern cares about results, too, but they may also be concerned about looking good and not making mistakes. Listen for phrases like "My boss said X is really important" or "I know my boss really wanted to make sure the agency offers Y." You can also just ask them what's most important to their manager. Armed with this information, adjust your presentation to give them talking points they can repeat to their boss.

ACE IN THE HOLE

If you can't get a decision maker to attend the presentation, record the pitch so they can watch it later.

THE IT ENGINEER

As the name implies, these are your technical wizards. Even though they care about how long you've been in business and whether they can trust you and all factors of a purchasing decision, when it comes down to it, they'd rather talk about how you're going to fix their SEO problem using JSON-LD to implement schema markup (whatever that means).

Talking shop is the IT engineer's way of assessing whether you know your shit and seem legit. It's also the reason you need to have sales engineers. If you yourself can't speak to the deep technical aspects of your services when an IT engineer is in the presentation meeting, you HAVE to have a technical person from your team there to talk the talk.

Your salesperson needs a solid understanding of the services you offer so that if they encounter this buyer type, they don't blow the deal before you've had a chance to get the real tech nerds in the room together. I use the label *nerds* in the best possible sense, as in people who are passionate about their craft. We're all nerds when it comes to our fascinations in life.

THE NUMBER CRUNCHER

The number cruncher could be a CFO, a partner at a private equity firm, the owner, or just an analytical, number-focused marketing professional. The point is that this person cares deeply about the numbers, and although they are assessing you on a variety of factors, they really want to hear about ROI estimates and your spreadsheet-focused analysis.

Even though it's unlikely many CFOs will actually attend your calls, your contact might mention them as part of the decision-making team. I've already coached you to have ROI- and results-related slides in your deck, so you should be covered.

Just know that these human calculators speak a particular language that essentially goes like this: "If I pay you $1, I need to get back $10. Prove to me that you can do that and let me know by when." This approach is called pencil selling, and it's also important when you're selling newer services.

For example, when I first started selling paid search services back in 2004, because it was very new, most of the prospects I spoke with had never done paid search advertising. Before I could sell them on my agency, I had to sell them on the idea of doing paid search in the first place. If you're selling a new kind of service or selling to someone who's never used the tactic you're pitching, pencil selling can become even more important than usual.

With some prospects, showing the numbers is the most important part of the pitch. This can be true even for services not directly or obviously connected to the money, such as technical website development.

THE OWNER/CEO

This is one of the buyer types you'll encounter most frequently, especially if you sell to smaller companies. There are more kinds of owners than I can cover in this book. You've got older owners who come from the old school. Younger hotshots who are digitally savvy. Some owners used to be marketers, whereas others used to be schoolteachers or doctors. It's really all over the board. Regardless of which flavor of owner/CEO you're speaking with, the main things they tend to care about are not getting screwed again, not making the wrong decision, and ROI projections. Of all the buyer types, the owner is the one that most needs the full monty (minus the deep technical info if they're not technically oriented).

THE SUPER-MEGA GLOBO CVP

These buyers are your CMOs, VPs, and high-level marketing managers at larger or enterprise-level organizations. They tend to speak in acronyms and corporate mumbo jumbo, saying things like, "We need to create a strategic, AI-driven interdepartmental synergy that will prevent MEGO" (my eyes glazing over, which mine did as I was typing that nonsense).

If you come from a corporate background, you understand how to talk to these people. If you don't have much corporate experience, talk less, listen more, and keep your approach on the formal side. Although you don't have to speak in corporate tongues or abandon your charming personality, understand that their world might be a bit different from your agency, which may have a Ping-Pong table, dogs roaming around, and a keg on tap in the break room.

SALES SKILL #2: MIRROR THEIR STYLE

Why are people afraid of even nonpoisonous spiders and

snakes? The main reason is because those creatures are so unlike us in appearance. Scientific research has shown that we have an affinity for people who are similar to us in appearance, style, energy, and/or background.

The first skill was about identifying the type of person you're selling to. Skill #2 is about what you do with that information. And it's pretty simple. If the main decision maker talks fast and likes to get to the point quickly, do your best to match and mirror their pace. If you've got an analytical number cruncher on the call, speak their language by highlighting the numerical parts of your presentation. If they say ROI a lot, you say ROI a lot.

Mirroring is simply matching your presentation to their speaking style, learning style, and areas of focus. Speaking like your prospect increases their affinity for you and their trust in what you're saying. That's why listening is such an important sales skill. To do what's taught in this chapter, you must first listen. Only then can you respond in a way that will resonate.

SALES SKILL #3: CALLBACK TO THEIR PERSEVERATION

In comedy, a callback is a joke that refers to one the comedian told earlier in the set. The purpose of callbacks is to make the audience feel a sense of familiarity with the material and with the comedian. Callbacks create audience rapport.

In psychology, perseveration refers to a situation where a person keeps repeating the same word, phrase, or gesture over and over again, even after the circumstances that prompted the thought or behavior are no longer in place. Psychologically speaking, the person is stuck.

If you recall, one of our key diagnosis questions was "What changed or happened in your business that caused you to reach out at this time?" Usually, some specific event or series of events causes the prospect to decide today is the day to get some help with their marketing problems.

The triggering event, along with the prospect's role and personality type, often causes them to perseverate on one or more core needs. Sometimes it is subtle, and sometimes it is screaming at you. If their last agency screwed up and overspent their online advertising budget, they may mention this pain point over and over and over again. Listen for elements of your services that they focus on compulsively. When you identify a perseveration, build slides about it into your presentation so you can call back to it as you go.

For example, if a prospect said during the discovery call, "I hate it when agencies don't proactively come to me with the latest SEO strategies," you're going to call back to that. Maybe you have a slide about this topic and you say something like, "During the discovery call, you mentioned how several other agencies were not proactive in the development and implementation of SEO strategy. Here is how we stay on top of Google algorithm updates."

Calling back to their perseveration is simple yet powerful. It may sound like I'm coaching you to be a slimeball salesman by playing with their head. I'm not. I'm coaching you to listen intently, acknowledge the tension they feel, and show them how you can relieve their tension. As long as you do it authentically and honestly, it's a win for both sides. The prospect feels heard and more likely to accept your suggested solution, which they truly need and want.

SALES SKILL #4: ADVANCED STORYTELLING AND CONNECTING TO THE CASH

Storytelling is often the best way to get prospects to understand and remember your key messages. Note that you don't tell stories only with your speaking; you tell them through visually appealing slides, too.

There is a specific kind of storytelling technique that is critical to all parts of your presentation but especially important when you are presenting insights and opportunity slides. The tactic is telling substories within the main story.

As a quick review, here is the main story you're telling throughout the sales process and in particular during the formal presentation.

> Sherry, you are at point A and you want to get to point C. Our agency services are B, the best way to get from point A to point C.

> Example: Your site currently generates ten leads per month, and you want to increase leads to twenty per month. Social media advertising is the best strategy to achieve your goal, and we're the best option for you to accomplish that goal.

Now let's cover the advanced storytelling technique, which

I call connecting to the cash. Although there are a variety of motivations prospects bring to their buying process (getting a good deal, impressing their boss, not getting burned again, etc.), the bottom-line reason is the bottom line.

At the end of the day, all anybody really cares about when buying digital marketing services is whether they will work. Will you make me more money than I pay you? Will you increase my sales at a profitable rate? You need to show them the money. As you are telling the tale about how you're the best option, you need to tell substories that connect to the cash.

First, a general, agency-level example:

Average Story:

"We specialize in working with software companies just like you."

Ace Story:

"We specialize in working with software companies just like you. Because we deal with the exact issues you're facing day in and day out, we've developed a proprietary process proven to produce the sales results you want faster than typical agencies can. Let me show you two specific examples."

Now let's look at two examples of cash-connected stories for sales engineering insights, the part of your presentation during which you'll use this technique the most.

Average Story:

"We audited your analytics account and noticed that the rate at which visitors return to your website is lower than we'd expect. That's an opportunity for improvement."

Ace Story:

"We audited your analytics account and noticed that the rate at which visitors return to your website is lower than we'd expect. Return visitors make up only 20 percent of your traffic. For a site like yours that sells expensive, high-consideration products, we'd expect that number to be closer to 50 percent.

"Based on additional analysis, we believe that the way you have products displayed on your home page is part of the problem. In particular, you don't have any products shown above the fold. We have several techniques that have been proven to increase new user engagement and sales by at least 10 percent. In your case, a 10 percent increase in web sales would translate into $10,000 in additional revenue per month."

Average Story:

"We noticed your paid search campaigns are using a lot of broad match keywords, which is not a best practice."

Ace Story:

"Your campaigns are using a lot of broad match keywords. Although broad match has its place, here is a screenshot of a query report for the last twelve months that shows these broad match keywords triggered ads for 'free calendar software.' You spent (i.e., wasted) $4,500 on those clicks.

"This other screenshot shows your 'sales tools' ad group is converting at a profitable rate, but the budget set for those keywords is too low and your ads are showing up only 60 percent of the time. Cleaning up the broad match problem is critical, but even simply moving that $4,500 of wasted budget over to the sales tools campaign would result in approximately $15,000 worth of additional sales each month without increasing your advertising budget."

The point is to connect the dots all the way back to their main motivation, which is to make more money. Here is a simple formula that most of your sales engineering substories should follow:

1. Here is a problem we found.
2. Here is why it matters and what it means for your business.
3. Here is how we solve that problem.
4. Here is how much money you will make.

You might not be able to attach a number to each individual insight. Having a total ROI estimate for your insights as a whole works just fine. As long as you follow the basic format of "here is a problem AND here is the financial benefit you'll get by fixing it," you've told a cash-connected story.

If you use subject matter experts to present the insights and opportunities slides, make sure they understand this formula. Unless the prospect is very well versed in what you're presenting, the sales engineers should not assume that the prospect understands how insights connect to the cash. They have to make the connection explicit.

As we discussed in the last chapter, you should tell all of these stories verbally. Don't use a ton of text writing them out. Your slide should have a screenshot or image related to the topic and a few words to help you remember the story you want to tell.

Brian   1:29 PM ☆ ↰ ⋮
to me ▾

Hi, Forrest,

Terrific presentation with great insights/identified opportunities—and the data to back them up. Nice to see a firm that understands how this all should tie back to achieving business goals rather than simply focusing on tactics.

Unsolicited email from a prospect showing the impact of connecting your stories to the prospect's bottom-line business goals.

Although cash-connected stories about specific insights can be powerful and believable on their own, to truly help you close deals, they must be integrated into the larger story about why the prospect should believe that your agency is the best choice. Here is the broader context your substories must fit within:

- We specialize in exactly what you need, so we are the option most likely to produce the results you want.
- We showed you proof from third parties that we're good at the service you need.

- We showed you specific insights that outline the opportunities you have.
- We proposed services that are designed to take advantage of those exact opportunities.
- We offered you fair pricing and set proper expectations regarding results and timing.
- We included case studies and other supporting information.
- We expressed our sincere desire to work with you and asked for your business.

SALES SKILL #5: SETTING AND KEEPING A GOOD PACE

I tend to present fast. Faster is not always better, but slowness can be a sales killer.

If you use my presentation structure, your pitch decks will tend to be on the longer side, possibly much longer than you're used to. Don't bore your audience by presenting them too slowly.

I generally coach people to keep things moving. I've presented a hundred slides in forty-five minutes and had people love it because the slides and stories were visually appealing, focused on specific opportunities for their business, and actionable in nature.

If you're moving at a good pace, presentations for one core service should take about thirty to forty-five minutes, including time for questions from the prospect. Two or more services could easily take sixty to ninety minutes, especially if the client is asking a lot of questions and/or the services are complicated.

Let clients ask questions anytime they want during a presentation. Stay conversational, not robotic. However, remember that you are running the show. You have to make sure you hit all the key parts of the story you're trying to tell. If someone asks a question early on about something that you cover later in the deck, assure them you'll be getting to that topic in just a few minutes. Answer pressing questions, but keep the action and the story moving forward.

These are general guidelines. Most importantly, match the pace and style of your prospect.

ACE IN THE HOLE

Pause occasionally and check in with your prospects by asking a question such as, "Bill, is the benefit of what I just covered clear to you?" If you have more than one person in the meeting, use a specific person's name so they know you expect a response from them. Besides making sure you're getting your message across, checking in from time to time keeps people engaged and listening to your presentation.

SALES SKILL #6: USING HUMOR AND CUSTOMIZING YOUR DECK FOR LAUGHS

Scientific studies have shown that shared laughter makes people feel closer to each other.

Humor is a super-powerful sales tool, if you are funny. If you're not naturally funny or witty, it can quickly become a cringeworthy deal killer. When in doubt, leave the humor out. Think fun over funny, or just tell an interesting story.

I happen to be naturally funny, or so I'm told. So I use humor quite a bit to great effect. A quick quip at just the right moment can loosen the prospect up and build some serious rapport. I've had prospects literally gasping for air on the other end of the phone because they were laughing so hard. When that happens, they almost always become clients.

What if you're not naturally funny? Not to worry, I have a way you can insert humor into your presentations while greatly minimizing the chances of crickets when you deliver your zinger.

The technique is to insert a funny picture, meme, or other humorous piece of information into the pitch deck itself. Make sure it's relevant to the prospect or situation. This allows you time to create something funny ahead of time and run it by others before you do it live, which greatly reduces the pressure on your delivery. The deck tells the joke more than you do. It's similar to you showing a friend a funny YouTube video. You did not make a funny video, but you created shared laughter, nevertheless. Here is a simple example.

I once had a client refer me to his fiancée, who was the marketing manager at a well-known women's fashion brand. When I was preparing the presentation deck, I went on LinkedIn and grabbed the headshot of my client. I stuck his picture on the slide that had our third-party credibility and added a funny caption. Here is a reenactment of what the slide looked like (that's not a picture of the actual client).

This took two minutes to add to a standard slide. Unexpectedly seeing a picture of her fiancée in a sales presentation made the prospect laugh and built rapport. But I didn't just do it for laughs. The image and caption was a reminder of the referral from someone she trusted, a callback to third-party proof that we might be the best choice. Big impact from a little laugh.

Key Point: Do not insert humor just to be funny. It should be relevant, too.

Although I'm not a professional comedian, lucky for us, my friend Jay Mays (who helped us with our diagnosis questions in chapter 4) was a professional stand-up comic AND a top sales pro in the digital services world. He started a company called Pitch Lab, which teaches business professionals how to use the principles of stand-up comedy to build their confidence and improve the delivery of their presentations. The Pitch Lab curriculum helps you differentiate yourself from the competition, build stronger relationships, and win more deals. If you'd like more infor-

mation on Pitch Lab or to speak with Jay, please visit www.
pitchlab.io.

SALES SKILL #7: THE NO-BULLSHIT ZONE: ON CURSING AND PROFESSIONALISM

Scientific studies have shown that swearing is a sign of more, not less, intelligence. If you have a particular skill, that is. There's always a fucking catch. See what I did there? ;-)

A study conducted by psychologists at Marist College found that verbal fluency was positively correlated with fluency in using obscene or taboo language.[5] So in some situations, if you are generally articulate and have a strong vocabulary, using a swear word at just the right time can loosen up the conversation, make it more authentic, and create rapport with the prospect. Remember the buyer types we discussed in chapter 9? Knowing what type of person you're speaking with can help you determine if using a choice word is the right choice.

So you may be wondering, can I say the word *ass* during my presentations? Is "fuck" off limits? Just how low can I go?

First, I'm not saying that swearing is a guaranteed winner in any sales scenario. What I am doing is pointing out a

5   Kristin L. Jay and Timothy B. Jay, "Taboo Word Fluency and Knowledge of Slurs and General Pejoratives: Deconstructing the Poverty-of-Vocabulary Myth," *Language Sciences* 52 (2015): 251–59, https://www.sciencedirect.com/science/article/pii/S0388000114001511X. Richard Stephens, "Swearing Is Actually a Sign of More Intelligence - Not Less - Say Scientists," ScienceAlert.com, February 2, 2017, https://www.sciencealert.com/swearing-is-a-sign-of-more-intelligence-not-less-say-scientists.

potential tool in your toolbox and giving you some guidelines for when you can use it effectively and when you shouldn't touch it with a ten-foot pole.

Second, there is a difference between using mild swear words for linguistic effect, to get a laugh, or build rapport and being truly obscene or nasty. Under no circumstances should you use racial slurs or say anything truly offensive. Hopefully, I did not even need to write that sentence.

Let me give you a few situations in which you might choose to throw a colorful word into the mix.

If you sense the prospect you're speaking with curses in everyday conversation (or actually curses first), you can create a bit of a bond by matching their speaking style. Only do this if it's comfortable. Just because they curse does not mean you have to.

Being authentic and real during a sales conversation is refreshing. Prospects in buying mode are on guard, especially if they've been burned by other agencies. Sometimes, speaking a bit less formally can make the conversation feel like one with a friend they can trust. When you sense using a particular swear word is going to make the conversation more comfortable, impactful, or funny, go for it.

Even though society seems to have become more accepting of cursing over the last few years, most people still do not curse in professional settings, especially not when speaking with unfamiliar salespeople outside of their organization. As such, when used correctly *and sparingly*, colorful language can be a subtle way to differentiate yourself from your competitors. The other agency is filled with stuffy professionals who don't fit the prospect's culture, but you are a regular Joe or Jane who can run with their crew.

Let me give you an example of a swear word that worked wonders for one of my clients and once again helped me build humor right into the pitch deck.

We used a slide similar to the one shown below.

First of all, it's visually funny and usually got a laugh before anyone said anything about it. Second, it's relevant. This was inserted as the second slide in the presentation decks, and I had a story about it.

> We speak to a lot of prospects just like you who have been burned by other agencies. So we just want to let you know right up front, we're entering the No-Bullshit Zone. That means we're going to be transparent and tell it like it is. We're not interested in bullshitting our clients. We want to set

realistic expectations and be honest about what's working and not working.

Besides getting a laugh, it had a real impact in several other ways. For starters, it sent a message in the first minute of the presentation that this is not going to be like any other presentation. It built rapport and instantly engaged prospects. Also, it helped prospects feel free to be honest with us about what was important to them, which gave us a better sense of how to meet their needs during the sales process and once they become a client.

Prospects would often refer back to the no-bullshit zone later in the presentation because it was so memorable. We even had clients refer to it a year after the original presentation. They'd say things like, "Hey, are we still in the no-bullshit zone? I need to discuss something with you."

If you feel uncomfortable cursing or if you sell into industries that are very buttoned up, just forget this section. You don't have to curse or make jokes to be successful at sales. I just wanted to provide a bit of insight to readers who like to speak with a bit of spice.

SALES SKILL #8: SETTING UP THE CLOSE

The next chapter is all about how to close the deal. As I've said in other parts of the book, you need to sell and close each step in the process. You need to sell the value of the diagnosis call, the value of the sales engineering audit, the value of the presentation, and so on. As Alec Baldwin taught us in *Glengarry Glen Ross*, "A-B-C. A, always; B, be; C, closing. Always be closing!"

There is one slight exception, and that is at the end of the formal sales pitch. Although we will show you some soft closing questions to use right at the end of the presentation, if you're selling reasonably high-priced services (say, $3,000–$7,500 for monthly management fees), most prospects are not going to say yes right at the end of the presentation. They may still have pitches scheduled with other agencies they are considering or need to "talk it over with the team."

Instead of truly trying to close the deal, we set up the close with a simple statement such as, "Barbara, for what it's worth, I want to let you know that after speaking with you and completing the audit, we feel strongly that we can help you achieve your goals, and we'd love to work with you. From our perspective, you seem like a perfect fit. If you decide you'd like to move forward, the next step would be to send you a formal agreement for your review. What do you see as the next step on your end?"

They'll usually respond with something like, "That was a great presentation. I need to talk it over with the team, and I'll get back to you next week."

There are more specific setups and closing techniques that

you can use right at the end of the presentation, which we'll cover in the next chapter, but the example above is a great way to end the presentation and transition to the final close.

If you've presented well and gotten a good reaction, you're almost done. But it's not over until the check clears the bank. Stay focused and get the ball across the goal line before you spike it. (Sorry, it's a sales book; I had to throw in a few sports analogies.) The closing tactics we cover in the next chapter will help you seal the deal.

KEY TAKEAWAYS FROM CHAPTER 9

- The system you're learning can do a lot of heavy lifting, but you still need to develop core sales skills to produce great results.

- Identify buyer type by asking questions and listening. Then adjust your presentation style to the prospect's learning style. Focus on meeting them where they are.

- Study and practice the eight sales skills covered in this chapter.

- Internalize the core sales story about how your services will produce the financial results your prospects crave, and be sure to tell that story over and over throughout your presentation.

- Set up the final close with a direct statement about your ability and desire to help the prospect.

CHAPTER 10

CLOSING LIKE AN ACE WITHOUT FEELING LIKE A SLIMEBALL

"To give real service you must add something which cannot be bought or measured with money, and that is sincerity and integrity."

—DONALD A. ADAMS

The golden rule states that you should "do unto others as you would have them do unto you," which implies that other people would like to be treated the way that you would like to be treated.

Dr. Tony Alessandra created an alternative to the golden rule, the platinum rule. The platinum rule states that we should "treat others *the way they want to be treated.*" The platinum rule takes into consideration the feelings and needs of others. The focus of the relationship shifts from "this is what I want" to "let me first understand what you want, and then I'll give you that."

This is not to say that your needs and your agency's needs are not important. In fact, they are equally important as the prospect's needs. However, nobody likes to be "closed." I only use the word in this book because it is part of the common sales lexicon and it is important to have a closing mindset.

So what do prospects want when it comes time to close the deal? Honesty, authenticity, and confidence that you are the best choice.

The clichés about closing include the greasy used car salesman who will say anything to seal the deal (i.e., lie); the cheesy closing techniques peddled in books and sales training throughout the '70s, '80s, and '90s; and the slick salesman who charms you into buying services you don't really need.

When I talk about closing, I'm not talking about any of that. In fact, if you've followed the advice in this book, by this point in the process, you have demonstrated powerful positioning and backed up your claims of unique value with a professional and engaging presentation that makes you the clear choice. You should have rock-solid confidence that you're playing a Winnable Game, which makes closing as easy and natural as providing the prospect with an *invitation* to enjoy the benefits you've promised. If you don't feel this way, you messed up or skipped a step along the way.

THE AUTHENTIC ACE AND THE FRICTION-FREE CLOSE

Closing is a deliberate act with real intention behind it. You need to have a closer's mentality. That said, closing should only be attempted when you have a genuine belief that you can help the client.

Intentional? Yes.

Direct? Absolutely.

Simple? No doubt.

Awkward, tricky, or high pressure? Never.

Although it's not common, I have had plenty of prospects say, right after I finish the last presentation slide, "Looks great. Let's do it." More often than not, there are few more hoops to jump through before you start cashing checks and sipping tropical drinks on the beach.

The basic closing formula shown below is friction-free. Use your own words so it fits your style. I'll provide examples throughout this chapter.

1. We showed you an opportunity to improve your results.
2. We are uniquely qualified to help you take advantage of that opportunity.
3. You're a perfect fit for our skills, and we'd love to work with you.
4. Are you ready to move forward?

People always want to know exactly what to say. The basic formula is to simply remind them why you can help them and ask if they want to move forward. It's no more complicated than inviting a friend to a party. You mention all the great stuff that will happen at the party, and then you ask them if they want to attend. That's it.

Although closing should be simple, there can be some sticking points before a prospect is ready to sign on the dotted line. Let's cover a bit of process as well as a few techniques that can take your closing (i.e., invitation) skills to the next level. Along the way, we'll address common obstacles you may have to navigate to get the final signature.

THE ONE MEETING YOU CAN'T MISS

If you're in sales and you don't already have a ton of meetings every week, you will once your marketing kicks in. As your system ramps up, you'll consistently have to manage many deals at various stages in your process. Although you don't want to chase ghosts (more on that in a minute), it's critical that you follow up consistently. Not annoyingly but consistently.

People get busy. Other priorities come up. Circumstances change. Strategies shift. As such, we need to stay near the top of the prospect's task list to make sure the ball gets across the goal line.

One simple yet important part of the process is to set a weekly meeting with yourself that you will never miss. Set aside one hour each week on whatever day works for you to follow up with and/or review every active deal in your pipeline. I find Tuesdays or Wednesdays to be the best as people are kind of crazy on Mondays and trying to get out the door on Fridays.

Although it may take you only twenty or thirty minutes each week, it's a good idea to block off an hour in case you get a response that requires you to jump on a call to complete the close.

All you have to do during this meeting with yourself is open up your pipeline (in your CRM, spreadsheet, or wherever you keep your list of open deals), go through each one, and take the appropriate action. Some deals may require no action because the prospect told you they were going on vacation for two weeks. Some deals may require a quick email to check in, while others may require a phone call or sending the prospect a client reference or case study you promised.

Can't I use tasks and calendar reminders? Do I really have to do this meeting every week? Yes and yes. You can and should use a task list and any other tools that help you stay on track. However, the weekly meeting does a few things that a task list or calendar can't do:

- It makes sure no deal falls through the cracks. Because

you're looking at every deal every week, they all stay fresh in your mind. If anyone ever asks you, "What's up with deal X?" you'll always know.

- It serves as a catchall. If you were in a rush after a meeting and forgot to jot down something you promised to send the prospect, by reviewing every deal, every week, you ensure that forgotten tasks don't languish for more than a few days.
- Your follow-up will be consistent. Although not every deal will require a weekly follow-up, the weekly meeting will make sure you don't skip the necessary follow-ups because of other priorities.

Consistent follow-up that is appropriate to the situation (i.e., not overkill and not needy) is critical to maintaining momentum and demonstrating your desire to work with the client. If you don't follow up, prospects may assume you don't care about their business. This is what I mean by having a closer's mindset: the intent and determination to get deals done without the slime.

One thing I've learned over the years is that a deal is never done until it's done. Even if a prospect says, with genuine excitement, "I love it. Let's do it," until the contract is signed and payment is made, it's not a closed deal. The weekly meeting helps you stay focused and in sales mode so you don't get cavalier and fumble the ball right before the goal line (sports analogy limit reached, I promise).

Set this weekly meeting with yourself and don't miss it. It's a simple yet important habit of top sales aces that takes only a few minutes a week but pays off in deals won.

THE ACE CLOSING QUESTION

Have you ever lost a sale for no apparent reason?

You built rapport, dazzled them with your presentation, got all the buy signals, and then bam, no deal.

What happened?

When you lose a deal you believe you should have won, it's usually because you failed to address one or more concerns lingering in your prospect's mind. There's a simple solution. It's a question you can ask that uncovers hidden deal killers so you can address them and close the deal. Even though you won't win every deal, this closing question will put you in the best possible position. At the very least, you'll never be left wondering what happened.

Ask this question at the end of your sales presentation:

"Jim, I know you probably have to talk this over with your team, so I'm not asking for a yes or no right now. However, I am confident that our solution is perfect for you, and we'd love to work with you. Is there anything I said or did not say that would prevent you from moving forward? If so, I'd like to address any lingering issues right now."

You'll get one of two answers.

Either the prospect will say, "Nope, it all sounds great. Let's do it" (at which point, you shut your mouth and send them the agreement), or they'll say something like, "Well, I liked X and Y, but I'm a bit concerned about A and B."

Since your goal is to cover everything in the presentation, any concerns a prospect raises at this point may surprise you. Here are three common issues to be ready for.

"You mentioned X, but I'm not really clear what that is or why I need it."

Clarify what you meant, and be sure to connect the benefit of X to their desired outcome (more leads and sales).

"It all sounds great, but I'd like to see a few more examples of your work."

When you hear something like this, the prospect is not 100 percent convinced you'll deliver on your promises or has some other concern. Since this type of statement can be a brush-off or a stall tactic to hide their true discomfort, you need to ask follow-up questions to clarify their exact concerns. Once you better understand what's behind their statement, provide relevant examples and responses. If appropriate, you can offer to connect the prospect with a couple of references.

"I did not hear you say anything about X, and that's important to me."

Be sure you understand their context before you respond. Ask them why X is important. Once you really understand their motivation for mentioning something they perceive to be missing, provide a relevant response and ask them if that resolves the issue.

Until a prospect says, "Let's do it," assume they're not ready to buy and ask your version of the closing question. If you keep hearing the same concern from multiple prospects, that's a clue that you need to adjust your presentation to deal with the recurring issue.

This one simple question will help you tie up any loose ends. Then, if you have not already done so, you can ask the final question, which would be something like, "We're ready to move forward with you. What do you see as the next steps?" or "At this point, how do you feel about moving forward with us?"

If they say they need to talk with their team or think it over, let them know you're in no rush and ask them when they'd like you to follow up. That's it. As I mentioned earlier, after doing a great diagnosis call and delivering a great presentation, closing should be as easy as inviting friends to a dinner party and knowing some people will say yes and some will say they can't make it. Intend for a yes, but be unattached to the outcome of any particular invitation.

Intention + Detachment = A Confident Close

Being needy and clingy in dating turns people off. Same with selling. Being attached to winning a particular deal can cause anxiety and make your sales performance feel forced and desperate. The solution is to be detached.

Yes, you're playing to win, but you're not desperate. You've done the work I've taught in this book. You're well positioned. You're playing Winnable Games. So you're going to do your best and let the chips fall where they may. Go into every sales interaction with the mentality that you win some and you lose some. Don't start counting your commissions. Do the work. Do your best, and over time, you'll win more than you lose.

The true definition of cool is being calm, confident, and non-needy, and that's attractive to prospects.

CAN YOU WORK WITH ME ON PRICE? HOW TO NEGOTIATE YOUR FINAL FEES AND DISARM LAST-MINUTE LAND MINES

If a prospect asks you to lower the fees you proposed, how you respond depends on how you determined your pricing and a few other factors. Before I get to the detailed scenarios and responses, I want to provide a simple four-step framework you can follow:

1. Acknowledge their request.
2. State your pricing policy.
3. Restate your unique value.
4. Restate the estimated return on investment.

Here are some common situations and effective responses.

Fixed Fees

If you have fixed fees that never change, your response is obvious. That said, you don't want to just give an abrasive no. So you can say something that's direct but a bit softer and reminds them of the value you offer.

"Jim, I understand everyone wants the best price. The services we proposed have fixed fees that never change for anyone. What I've shown you is the best price we offer. Hopefully, you saw the potential return on investment we estimated and can see that the results will far outweigh our fee."

Custom Solutions

If you come up with a custom price each time and you can't or otherwise don't want to lower your fee, you can use the same basic approach I described for fixed-fee proposals with a few modifications.

"Jim, I understand everyone wants the best price. Hopefully, you saw the potential return on investment we estimated and can see that the results will far outweigh our fee. I quoted you the best price we can offer to deliver the results you want and the excellent customer service you expect. Anything less is simply not profitable for us."

That last line about profitability usually stops them in their tracks. You are saying, in a nice and professional way, take it or leave it. No sane businessperson is going to argue that you should do a deal you'll lose money on. A respectfully delivered "take it or leave it" conveys confidence and cool detachment.

Extra Headroom

Another approach is to make your fees a bit higher than you need so you have room to lower them if the prospect asks for a discount. I don't generally recommend this approach as it can set a bad precedent. If you give a prospect a discount once, they will expect another one every time they need additional services. If you get into a discount cycle with a client, the only way out is to jack up your fees for each new service you present so that when they inevitably ask for a discount, you can lower your fee to what you would have charged in the first place.

Also, discounting can cause you to run into issues when a client refers a friend and you offer them different pricing for the same work. My general advice is not to get into this situation in the first place. Have a firm policy that once you set your fee, whether fixed or custom, that's the fee.

ACE IN THE HOLE

In contrast to my advice to set your fees and stick to them, if you are pitching a huge client on a big number, once your point of contact has made the decision to hire you, they may have to submit your contract to their legal and/or purchasing departments for final approval. CFOs and procurement people pride themselves on shaving costs off every deal. If you've done your due diligence during diagnosis, you'll know your point of contact's budget approval limit and whether final approval will involve other parties. If you know that a purchasing manager or CFO will be involved, you may want to proactively pump up your proposed price so you can give the corporate coupon clippers the win they need.

Multiple Service Discount

Prospects purchasing multiple services often ask if they can get a bulk discount. If you have real efficiency when a prospect buys multiple services, giving a discount may make sense to help close a deal.

However, for agencies that sell each marketing service as

its own scope of work, multiservice clients can actually require MORE work. If you have different teams delivering each service, a multiservice client may require more internal meetings and an additional account management layer.

The point is to know your business and profitability factors and respond accordingly.

Pay per Performance/Results

Even though it's not necessarily new, over the last three years or so, I've seen an uptick in prospects asking for pay-per-performance pricing. This means that your fee is tied to some key performance metrics, such as the number of leads or sales generated from your efforts. If you don't hit the goals, you get less money (or no money).

If your agency offers these types of fee arrangements and is successful with them, keep doing it. Offering pay-per-performance deals makes hiring your agency a no-brainer. However, in most cases, you should not offer pay-per-performance deals. Prospects typically ask for this type of fee arrangement because they've been burned by other agencies and they are looking for a guarantee that they will not be burned again.

Here is why you should stay away from pay-per-performance deals, unless your agency is truly set up to benefit from them.

First, the client is unfairly shifting the risk of owning and running a business to you. It's your responsibility to do a great job with whatever services you are hired to deliver and that's it. Everything else is the prospect's responsibility. It's their business and their risk, not yours.

Second, in most cases, a variety of factors beyond your control can impact your ability to produce results. For example, if you're running paid search ads and the client changes a bunch of URLs that you were sending traffic to but forgets to tell you and the paid search stats tank for the month, that is zero percent your fault and you should get paid in full for your time and work. And what if a new competitor comes along and offers a better product at a lower price than your client offers? I could go on and on with examples. The point is, there are usually way too many things beyond your control for pay-per-performance arrangements to be tenable.

Third, calculating and collecting your fees can quickly become a stressful nightmare and create uncertainty in your cash flow. Furthermore, if your marketing goes so well that the client ends up having to pay you way more than they would have had you simply delivered the services for a fair fee, you may inadvertently create a financial dynamic that causes resentment.

Unless you have a good reason, don't do pay-per-performance deals.

If someone asks for a pay-per-performance deal, just state that you don't offer those sorts of arrangements and use some of the reasons above to explain why. Then reiterate your sales engineering insights, your experience, and your unique value points as the reason they should trust you to do better than the last agency.

Make Your Life Simple: Just Say No to Discounts

Generally speaking, I recommend having a no-discount policy. I find that when you have the rock-solid confidence that comes from properly qualifying prospects, properly scoping the work, and knowing that your agency is great at what it does, you can respond to any discount request with a firm yet professional no. You'll actually close more deals, as your clients will respect you more, and your life will be much easier.

The important insight here is this: when you are at the end of the sales process and someone asks for a discount, they have almost certainly already decided to pick you, which means they already saw the value. So in most cases, it's pretty safe to call their bluff. Here is a real-life example.

I pitched a large manufacturing company on a conversion optimization project. All the sales calls went great, and I could tell they wanted to go with us. Right at the end, the buyer, who was a bit of a tough customer, said, "Forrest, we like your proposal, but you're three times more expensive than any of the other options we've looked at. Is there anything you can do on the price to help us out?"

Knowing that we were at the top of our game and almost certainly three times better than any other options he was looking at, I said, "Rob, I understand your request, but I believe our services provide far more value than the other options you're considering, and I know from years of experience that we are priced fairly for the level of expertise we offer. I'm sorry, but I can't reduce the price and remain profitable."

He said, "Okay, send me the contract."

Confidence. Closes. Deals. Even when you are the most expensive option.

Despite my general stance on discounts, there are two times when lowering your fee might make sense.

You Need the Business

There are times where you need the deal to keep the lights on. This is a shitty place for any business to be in, and you need to get out of it ASAP. That said, if you need gas money and a discount is the only thing standing between you and closing the deal, go for it. Just don't make it a habit as you can quickly cause severe burnout and send your business into a death spiral.

It's Worth It

Sometimes winning a particular deal offers value beyond your fee that makes it worth a discount. For example, I've sold SEO services to Amazon. Because being able to say "Amazon is a client and trusts our agency" helps me close other deals, there is real value beyond the fees they pay. Amazon did not ask for a discount, but if they had, I probably would have given them one. Even if it had significantly eaten into profit on that deal, I would have treated the discount as a "marketing expense."

Bottom line: Be quick to raise your fees and slow to lower them.

AGREEMENTS THAT SEAL THE DEAL AND CREATE EFFICIENCY

Although technically I could give you legal advice because I'm a licensed attorney, I'm not going to do that. It's beyond the scope of this book and I'm not your attorney. Instead, I'm going to give you general advice on how to structure your agreements to help you close deals and make the process of creating them quick and easy.

The main reason I'm even including this section in the book is because, as I mentioned earlier, the deal is not done until it's signed and the first payment is made. As such, the agreement you send is not merely a document with legal mumbo jumbo and some numbers and line to sign. It's a sales tool and an important part of your sales process. Or at least it should be.

In the system I've taught you, once a prospect asks for the formal agreement, you should have at least a 95 percent chance of closing. If you have a crappy agreement, your results may be lower. So let's not send a sloppy, confusing agreement but rather a professional, clear, and compelling one that reinforces the messages you've delivered along the way.

Here are the basic rules you should follow.

Make sure you choose a font that is easy to read and that your agreement is formatted and laid out in a professional manner. Even though your document does not need pretty pictures or graphic design, it should look just as professional as your website and your presentation deck.

If you sell multiple services or packages, write up a scope of work section for each service. If you can, make the scope of work sections 100 percent standard and static. If you sell custom programs, make the parts that are always the same static and leave spaces for you to fill in the custom details.

SUPER IMPORTANT: Don't shortchange the scope of work by making it too simple. Think of this section like the summary of your shopping cart on an e-commerce website. Your prospect is about to check out and give you their money, but they want to make sure they have the right stuff in their cart. If something is off, missing, or different from what you promised during the presentation, they are not going to sign. Instead, they are going to send you an email with questions about why the terms are different. One simple way to prevent this problem is to simply cut and paste the bullet points and information from your presentation right into the scope of work section.

On the other hand, don't make scopes of work unnecessarily long. Listing tons of "included" items is okay until people think you've padded the section with unnecessary work. If you throw in too many bells and whistles to try to build up the perceived value, prospects will sometimes ask you to remove things and then expect hefty discounts.

If appropriate, include a bit of language just after your scope of work section that discusses your onboarding and billing processes.

Last, you should have all the legal mumbo jumbo. It should be its own section that refers back to the scope(s) of work. It's akin to having a master services agreement with an attachment. Each scope of work stands on its own terms but is governed by the broader legal terms.

The sections of your agreement could look like this:

1. Intro letter or cover sheet
2. A half or full page of awards or other unique value reminders (keep it simple)
3. Scope of work (or multiple SOWs if you are selling services à la carte)
4. Legal terms and conditions that incorporate the scope(s) of work
5. Signature page
6. Any other necessary attachments

However you do it, remember that the agreement is an extension of your agency and your brand. It's just as important as all the other assets you use to market and sell your services. Give it the time and effort it deserves so it represents your agency well and reinforces the buyer's confidence that you are the best option.

SECRET WEAPON: EMAIL CLOSING

When selling digital marketing services, you'll often get last-minute questions and requests via email.

The last moments before closing a deal are often the most emotional for both buyer and seller. You are salivating at the thought of closing a deal, and the prospect, although convinced you're the right option, may still be nervous and concerned about making the wrong decision. That's where email closing comes in.

If at the last minute the prospect asks about something substantive or emotional, such as a discount or major change to the scope of work, it may be best to respond via email. I've closed many deals this way.

Email (as opposed to the phone) allows me to take my time to craft a response that addresses their issue in a professional and well-reasoned manner. It also allows me to run my response by my team to make sure I've included accurate information, and I can reinforce points from the presentation that I might forget to mention on an emotional phone call. Furthermore, email allows me to stay cool and convey confidence in my response, especially when I have to say no to a prospect's request.

All that said, there is a time to pick up the phone. That time usually comes when the response is a bit complicated or not easily conveyed via written communication. There are no hard-and-fast rules here. It's about how you're feeling. If the prospect is a bit antsy and you feel that getting them on the phone is the best way to set their mind at ease, by all means, pick up the phone. Have an authentic conversation to remind them you're the good guy and you're here to make them feel as comfortable as possible.

Sometimes I write an email response to organize my thoughts but never send it. After writing the email, I realize I need to just pick up the phone, and I use the draft to make sure I cover everything I need to cover to close the deal.

THE CONFIDENT CLOSE

Quite a few prospects, especially ones that have been burned before, have a dismissive attitude toward agencies. Burn victims may think that because they will be paying you money, they have complete control of the situation and that you, the lowly agency sales scum, should bow down, do whatever they say, and beg for their business.

Also, less experienced and less confident salespeople may put themselves in a submissive position by default. In order to close with confidence, you need to shift the power dynamic. Here are some steps you can take.

Do the Work to Be a Great Agency

If you or the ownership of your agency has not taken the time to assemble great processes and hire employees who deliver great results, then you have no reason to be confident when selling.

You must position yourself as uniquely qualified to produce the results AND actually able to live up to that positioning. Your agency does not have to be the absolute best in the world, but it needs to at least be substantially above average. If you own or work for an agency that is not great or willing to become great, I suggest you dust off your résumé. Sales skills, like marketing skills, can't fix fundamental business problems.

Remember Who You Are

Assuming your agency is actually good at what it does, the next step is to remind yourself of a few things. You are the doctor and they are the patient. They have pain and you have the relief they desperately want. Your agency is good at what it does and you know it.

Remind yourself that you're on equal footing with the prospect. Although a prospect will give you money if they become a client, you and your team will give them your time, expertise, and hopefully the results they want. At worst, it should be an even trade. At best, knowing that most agencies are at or below average, you're in control. You may be one of only a few agencies that can really deliver what they need.

Price Fairly

Again, if your agency is good at what it does, offers some unique benefits, and is priced fairly, you have everything you need to adopt a "take it or leave it" attitude. That's not a license to be arrogant, just confident.

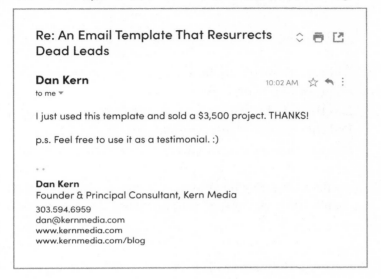

Although I don't generally believe in magic bullets, using proven techniques can help you grow your sales more quickly than trial and error. That's pretty much the whole point of this book.

I'm going to teach you a simple technique right now that will save you time and produce better results. I developed the technique through trial and error over a long time. You will learn it in sixty seconds. That's the power of cloning an ace.

Have you ever had a hot prospect go silent for no apparent reason?

You wowed them with your presentation and were sure they were going to buy. They may have even said they were going to move forward.

Then, out of nowhere, they stopped responding.

What happened?

1. Did you overestimate how well you presented?
2. Did they buy from someone else?
3. Did they get busy with another project?
4. Did they have a family emergency?
5. Did they leave the company?

Regardless, you may be able to save the sale. And even if you can't, it's important to find out what went wrong so you can improve.

First, you have to get the prospect to respond.

Below is an email template that nearly always gets "dead" prospects to respond the same day, no matter how long it's been since you last heard from them.

Adjust the personal details as necessary, but don't change the subject line or the general structure.

Subject Line: Please Reply

[First Name]

Hope all is well with you.

I left you a voice mail and sent two emails over the last few weeks, but I've not received a reply.

The last thing I want is to be a pest.

Please reply to this email and let me know if you're still interested in continuing our conversation about how our services can help you [insert the result they want] or if I should take you off my follow-up list.

Thanks,

[Your Name/Signature]

Not only can you use this template to resurrect dead deals, but it can also work in any situation where someone you were communicating with ghosts you.

It's one of the few things I've ever developed that works nearly 100 percent of the time. Pretty much a magic bullet for getting people to respond.

You now know every part of the sales system I've perfected over the last seventeen years and most of the tips, tricks, and skills I use to produce record-breaking results. It's time to cover tracking and how to use tools, templates, and automation to maximize efficiency, scalability, and profitability.

KEY TAKEAWAYS FROM CHAPTER 10

- Follow the platinum rule and be authentic.

- You're not tricking people. You're inviting them to do business with you.

- Take a positive approach. Remember that you're offering to help solve someone's problems, not cheating them out of their money.

- Use the ace closing question to resolve the sales conversation one way or the other.

- Be prepared to negotiate final pricing and terms by educating yourself on common situations and establishing firm policies around discounting.

- The format and style of your agreements is just as important as any other part of your marketing and sales process.

- Confidence closes deals. If you've followed the entire system I've presented in this book, you know you are playing a Winnable Game, and that should give you the rock-solid confidence you need to close powerfully.

CHAPTER 11

TRACKING, TOOLS, AND TEMPLATES + AUTOMATION

"Efficiency is doing better what is already being done."

—PETER DRUCKER

On the night of July 16, 1999, John F. Kennedy Jr. accidentally crashed his Piper Saratoga plane into the Atlantic Ocean. He, his wife, and his sister-in-law perished. Because JFK Jr. was not qualified to fly by instruments, he was flying the plane visually. Unfortunately, familiar landmarks and the horizon were hard to see due to poor weather conditions and darkness.

Investigations into the crash found that Kennedy experienced spatial disorientation which made it nearly impossible for him to accurately interpret his position, altitude, or speed. Once a pilot becomes spatially disoriented, they experience illusions in their perception of the plane's motion and start to commit steering errors that send the aircraft into a "graveyard spiral."

Kennedy's plane crashed because he was trying to eyeball it in the dark.

Having insight into a machine's performance is critical for successful operation over the long term. Although you may not be a pilot, you need look no further than the dashboard of your car to understand the importance of having key metrics at your fingertips to ensure your system is running well and, when it's not, to be able to quickly identify problems and make course corrections.

You've worked hard to build a world-class sales system. Take the time to set up an appropriate tracking dashboard and learn how to use the feedback it provides to land safely at your desired destination.

Don't eyeball it in the dark.

SETTING UP A DASHBOARD TO TRACK AND REFINE YOUR SALES MACHINE

As I built and refined the system I've taught you in this book, I built a tracking and reporting dashboard that corresponds to all of the deal stages I covered in chapter 3.

Whatever you use to track your results, you need to track two main areas: lead attraction and sales performance. Although I mention them as two areas, in reality, they form one continuous flow from market qualified lead (MQL) all the way through to closed won.

Your tracking dashboard should answer three core questions.

WHAT ARE MY RAW NUMBERS?

In order to hit your overall sales goal(s), you need to have targets for each sales stage, and the first thing your dashboard must tell you is how you are doing in terms of raw numbers.

For example, if you have a goal of attracting ten sales qualified leads (SQLs) per month, you need to have a raw count of how many SQLs you actually received.

Below is a list of the raw numbers you should track. If it seems like a lot, don't fret. Your CRM or a handy spreadsheet I've created can do this automatically (get your free copy of SalesTracker™ at www.clonetheace.com).

- How many MQLs did we get this month?
- How many SQLs did we get this month?
- How many diagnosis meetings did we schedule this month?
- How many diagnosis meetings did we conduct this month?
- How many diagnosis meetings turned into fully qualified prospects?
- How many presentations did we deliver?
- How many contracts did we send?
- How many deals did we close?
- How much revenue did we generate?

Here is an example of part of the raw number dashboard from my SalesTracker™:

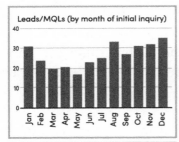

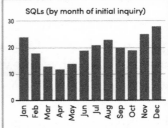

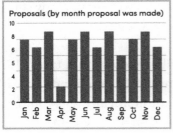

WHAT ARE MY CONVERSION RATES?

Next, you need to track conversion rates between each deal stage. This allows you to quickly identify leaks in your system.

For example, let's say you're hitting your lead attraction goals and getting enough SQLs into your pipeline. You're following up quickly and booking lots of diagnosis calls. However, your dashboard shows that only 40 percent of the people that book a diagnosis call actually show up. The 40 percent conversion rate between booking a meeting and actually conducting it indicates a problem at that point in your process. The results may be poor because you're being too lenient in your initial qualification or because your message about the value of the meeting is weak.

Although the conversion rate data may not instantly point

to the root cause of the problem, you will at least get a "warning light" that gives you a chance to further diagnose the problem in that part of your sales process and make course corrections to avoid a graveyard spiral.

Here is what your conversion rate dashboard might look like:

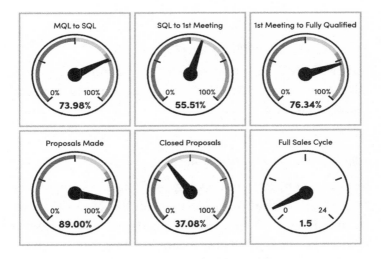

Although it's critical to know the rate at which leads convert from stage to stage, you need to be able to compare metrics that skip stages, too.

For example, the rate at which MQLs convert to SQLs, the next stage in your process, versus the rate at which MQLs convert all the way to a closed deal tell two different stories. Although no lead becomes a closed deal without passing through every stage of the process, the conversion rate from MQL to SQL is a direct measure of the quality of your leads. If you get ten MQLs a month but only five are SQLs, that indicates your marketing is effective at attracting prospects with potential to become a client only 50 percent of the time. On the other hand, the ratio of MQLs that turn into clients is a more general measure of the effectiveness of your sales process as a whole.

Below are few other nonsequential conversion rates to track and review on a regular basis.

MQLs to fully qualified prospects

This ratio tells you how effective your marketing is at attracting the right prospects. It's more a measure of lead quality than of sales skill.

SQLs to fully qualified prospects

By cutting out unqualified raw leads and starting at the SQL stage, this ratio tracks the health of both your marketing efforts and your sales skills. If this ratio is low, it may be because your marketing is attracting too many low-quality leads and you are being too lenient when classifying MQLs as SQLs. If this is happening, it may cause you to schedule diagnosis meetings with prospects who never really had a chance to become fully qualified.

Alternatively, a low ratio here could indicate an issue with your sales skills or process. For example, if you are getting high-quality leads but you are not selling the value of the diagnosis call and prospects are not showing up to the meetings, you are short-circuiting your chance to fully qualify high-quality prospects.

Fully qualified to closed deal

Assuming you're not being too lenient when classifying SQLs as fully qualified, this conversion rate is more specific to your sales skill as it cuts out the unqualified leads with whom you never had any chance of closing a deal. It's a ratio that focuses on your ability to shepherd truly qualified leads through your sales function to a closed deal. If you are talking to a good number of fully qualified prospects but the rate at which you close deals is too low, your presentation and other sales skills may be falling flat. Alternatively, a low ratio here could mean you have weak positioning that is causing you to be perceived as a generic brown package instead of the obvious best choice.

Proposals presented to closed deals

This ratio tells you how effective your presentations are at persuading prospects. If the ratio is low, you may have a presentation skill issue. Alternatively, a low score may indicate you are letting too many unqualified prospects make it to the proposal stage in the first place. You'll have to investigate to find the root cause.

When your tracking system allows you to calculate conversion rates between any two steps, whether sequential or not, you can assess the effectiveness of nearly any aspect of your sales process and identify areas for improvement. If you have multiple sales professionals on your team, you'll need to have a way to segment the data by person to evaluate each individual's performance.

WHAT ARE MY AVERAGES?

When you're looking at metrics month by month, you need the raw numbers because the raw numbers allow you to calculate your conversion rates. However, when you're looking for trends over longer periods or want to forecast future sales, you need averages.

Averages are useful in two main ways:

1. They can help you determine if you're hitting monthly goals rarely or consistently.
2. They can help you plan for growth. For example, if you know your one sales rep can handle twenty-five leads per month and you've been averaging forty per month for the last quarter or two, it may be time to hire a second salesperson.

Here are the averages you'll want to track. This list is similar to the list of raw numbers, with a few additions.

- Average MQLs per month
- Average SQLs per month
- Average diagnosis meetings scheduled per month
- Average diagnosis meetings held per month
- Average fully qualified prospects per month
- Average number of presentations delivered each month
- Average number of agreements sent each month
- Average sales cycle from lead to closed deal
- Average number of deals closed per month
- Average size of deals closed
- Average total revenue generated per month

Here is what the averages might look like on your tracking dashboard:

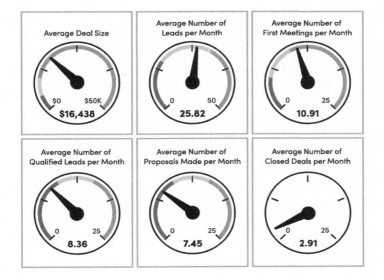

Tracking your numbers and making course corrections based on them is a critical component of a successful sales system. Another important factor in sales growth and scalability is efficiency throughout your system.

How to Be More Efficient

In 2015, an agency owner hired me to help him with an issue he was having in his sales process. It was taking upward of six hours to complete his sales engineering and create a scope of work for SEO presentations.

Once I began to diagnose the problem, it was clear that he also had a lot of other issues in his sales process. Almost all of these, including never being able to hire a good salesperson, could be traced back to a lack of consistent process. Without a consistent process, he was not able to fully leverage the efficiency that comes from tools, templates, and automation.

When I first got into sales full time, I would often manually repeat the same tasks over and over. For example, every time a lead came in, I would write, from scratch, basically the same email to get the prospect to schedule a diagnosis call. Besides writing each email, I had to check my calendar and include some dates and times I was available. Even though it took only about five minutes to write and send each email, I felt like I was wasting time. Because I was wasting time.

Eventually, I got smarter and I used my CRM to create an email template, which included merge fields for the prospect's first name and other common attributes. I started including a link in the emails to my calendar software that allowed prospects to select a time that worked for them without having to email back and forth for two days just to find a time.

Once I'd implemented these simple tools and templates, it took about thirty seconds to respond to a lead instead of five minutes. That's four minutes and thirty seconds saved per lead, which equaled almost 2.5 hours per month. You may already use a scheduling software and think "Big deal, Forrest." But keep in mind that this is just one example of how using tools, templates, and automations can save time and cognitive load on your brain. I guarantee there are at least some time and efficiency leaks in your current sales process.

I want you to become a bit obsessed, like I did, with employing tools and creating standard templates that will not only save time but also make it easier to hire average employees and still get solid productivity out of them. Let's explore a few additional ways you can increase the efficiency and effectiveness of your sales system.

TOOLS FOR BUILDING AND RUNNING YOUR PROCESSES

You can't respond to leads without an email system. You can't host a web presentation without web presentation software. You can't...You get the idea. Software and tools are the main parts of your sales machine. Let me show you another example of how a tool can save you time. Hat tip to Mike Belasco, the CEO of www.goinflow.com, for showing me this tool and concept.

The first step of the sales engineering process I installed in his agency (to solve the six-hour research problem) was an internal briefing meeting with the sales engineers. The point of this meeting was to go over what was uncovered on the diagnosis call so they could focus their research on the items most interesting to each prospect. These meetings often involved two or three team members plus the salesperson running the deal.

At a busy agency, it was hard to find forty-five minutes when everyone was free. Once the meetings were scheduled, they were not very efficient. Some team members had to sit through information that was relevant only to one person before getting to the information relevant to their service area.

Loom is a simple screen recording software. Mike suggested that we have the salesperson record a five- to ten-minute video describing the initial diagnosis call. The salesperson would then simply send a link to the video, and each team member could watch it at their convenience and skip to the parts that were relevant to them.

The idea of using a simple tool to have asynchronous meetings saved a ton of time and aggravation. Now, instead of the sales coordinator spending ten to twenty minutes trying to book a meeting with four people and each person spending thirty to forty minutes in the meeting, the admin spends zero time per meeting and each participant, including the salesperson, spends fifteen to thirty minutes less than they used to.

That's the power of tools.

Below is a list of the tools you'll likely need for a complete, efficient system, regardless of the size and complexity of your agency. Whether you have one Swiss Army knife or a set of individual tools that work together, you need a tool for each of the functions listed.

Note that I'm focusing only on the core selling function and not marketing. The toolset for marketing your agency is virtually endless and beyond the scope of this book.

(Also, please note the tools I'm recommending are relevant *now*. Technology moves quickly. Three years from now, there may be alternative options available.)

CLOUD-BASED EMAIL, DOCUMENTS, AND CALENDAR

For basic communication, key document storage, and management of the administrative side of your entire sales process. G-suite from Google is a popular choice.

CUSTOMER RELATIONSHIP MANAGEMENT (CRM)

For tracking and managing all of your contacts as they progress through each deal stage. Also, you may use your CRM to create and store templates, automate your email responses, and report on your sales metrics. If you're still using a spreadsheet, check out HubSpot's free sales CRM. Pipedrive is a solid and affordable option, too.

WEB PRESENTATION SOFTWARE

For holding your diagnosis calls and to conduct and record your sales presentations via screen share. If you have a limited amount of calls and participants, you can get by with free versions. Paid subscriptions provide time-saving advantages and additional features you may need. Zoom and UberConference are good options.

SALES ENGINEERING TOOLS

Sales engineering may require third-party software to audit client assets, such as a subscription to SEMRush to conduct SEO research. The tools you need depend on the services you offer.

Also, you'll likely need to access prospects' relevant website and marketing accounts (such as Google Ads, Google Analytics, and Search Console). Although you may not need to buy third-party tools to analyze existing marketing accounts, you may need to sign up for agency-level accounts to improve your efficiency. For example, consider getting a Google Ads Manager Account to manage all of your paid search clients in one place, rather than having to log in to each client's account directly.

INTERNAL COLLABORATION TOOLS

If you take a team selling approach, you may need tools to help you manage tasks such as sales engineering and your client onboarding process, as well as for internal communication. Software such as Slack, Trello, and Asana are popular choices.

E-SIGNATURE

For sending, electronically executing, and managing your agreements. Check out DocuSign, Adobe Sign, or eversign.

Having tools is essential, but you also need to employ templates to help you run your processes more efficiently.

TEMPLATES FOR FLAWLESS AND EFFECTIVE EXECUTION

Your sales system is made of processes that you execute. Templates are the nuts and bolts of your sales machine and help you run the machine effectively and efficiently.

If you're not familiar with the term in the context of a sales process, a template is simply a document or file with a preset format. Templates have three main benefits:

1. Templates save you time by eliminating the need to re-create documents that you use over and over. Examples include repetitive emails, standard slides in your pitch deck, and your formal service agreement.
2. Templates help you run your processes effectively by reminding you how to execute each step well. A well-designed diagnosis form with all the questions you need to ask is a great example.
3. Templates help you maintain consistency throughout your sales function, which makes it easier to hire, train, and scale and relieves the need to find high-priced sales aces.

I've created a variety of templates and examples for nearly every part of the system I've taught you in this book. You can view and download the following templates, with examples, at www.clonetheace.com:

- Ideal client profile worksheet
- Positioning worksheet
- Lead response email templates
- Diagnosis call template
- Presentation deck template
- Tracking and reporting spreadsheet (SalesTracker™)

AUTOMATIONS THAT ENHANCE PRODUCTIVITY AND REDUCE TIME TO RESULTS

Because it's a bit beyond my area of expertise, I'm not going to spend a lot of time going into technical detail about specific automations. That said, automating repetitive tasks can really save you time and help you drive more sales, so I want to touch on a few key points.

First, what should you automate? Here are four indicators that automation might be in order:

1. The task is repetitive.
2. The task is mostly administrative in nature (rather than substantive and strategic).
3. The task is completed digitally.
4. The task does not need a real human touch to be done well.

Some automations are obvious and easily handled by the tools you'll employ. You may already use some of them. Here are a few examples:

- Email autoresponders to form submissions from your website
- Cloud-based calendar system that allows prospects to schedule meetings
- Automated meeting reminders sent to prospects via email
- Contacts being entered into your CRM when they submit a form on your website

Some automations are a bit less obvious and may require some upfront configuration that goes beyond checking basic settings. The two examples below can increase your efficiency:

1. Configuring your tools to automatically create a new prospect folder with copies of all of your sales templates each time a prospect fills out a form on your website or is otherwise entered into your CRM system.
2. Configuring your CRM to automatically initiate the

sales engineering process in your prospect/project management software when a deal is moved from the Diagnosis Call Complete stage to the Qualified/Preparing Proposal stage.

Regardless of what you implement from this chapter, you should always be on the lookout for ways to increase your efficiency and effectiveness. You can do that by asking yourself the following four questions on a regular basis:

1. Are any warning lights flashing on my tracking dashboard? If so, what are the root causes and prescribed solutions?
2. Is there a tool that can make this task easier, faster, or better?
3. I notice I repeat a particular task over and over. Can I save time by creating a template for all or part of it?
4. Is there some way to automate this task so I don't even have to do it in the first place?

Bottom line? Be engaged, be on top of your pipeline, and be as efficient as you can. Leverage tracking, tools, templates, and automation to reduce the time a task takes for anyone involved in the sales process. In the final chapter, we're going to cover a few customizations you can make to ensure my system fits your specific situation.

KEY TAKEAWAYS FROM CHAPTER 11

- Don't fly blind. Set up a tracking dashboard to monitor and manage your sales system to stay on track to achieve your sales goals.

- Make sure your system tracks raw numbers, conversion rates, and averages across all deal stages.

- Use tools and templates to improve your efficiency and effectiveness.

- Look for opportunities to save time by automating tasks.

CHAPTER 12

CUSTOMIZE
THE CLONE

"You can't copy anybody and end with anything. If you copy, it means you're working without any real feeling."
—BILLIE HOLIDAY

This book makes two main arguments. The first is that you need a system with processes, tools, and templates. The second argument is that my system is proven to work and you can clone it to improve your results.

Although both of those statements are fundamentally true, they are not true without qualification. Cloning is a catchy and useful concept to use in a book title, and it's smart to apply lessons from someone who has been successful in your field. However, it's important that you understand, even in the world of biology, clones are not exact copies.

When you clone a human, it creates *genetically* identical twins. However, while the DNA of a clone may match the original's, the expression of the cloned genetics will not be identical to that of the original. People are more than a product of their genes. A real human clone would have its own personality, character, intelligence, and talents, just like identical twins do.

You cannot clone a person's mind, life circumstances, or environment. A person's experiences contribute to their traits. A cloned Hitler would not necessarily grow up to be a mass murderer, and being the twin of Mother Teresa does not guarantee you'd grow up to be a saint.

Similarly, even if your agency sells the same services to the same target market as another agency, the two agencies are not exactly the same. The core of your agency is made up of people, and every person has their own unique personality, past experience, and skillset.

I suggest you do your best to copy my system but in a way that fits your circumstances and style. Don't get wrapped up in doing everything exactly as I've described it. I want you to have the freedom and flexibility to express my system in your own way. Not only is that more realistic, but it also works better.

AUTHENTIC SELLING: BRING YOUR PERSONALITY TO THE PARTY

One of the fundamental values of the Clone the Ace Sales System is authenticity. In one sense, authenticity means being transparent and honest about your services and setting appropriate expectations. In another sense, authenticity is about being yourself and letting your personality animate the system.

A good clone is not a robot coldly executing its program but a real live human infusing its own unique style into its actions. You have to be believable. You have to be alive. Here are a few examples of how you can ensure you're being your authentic self.

IN PERSON VERSUS OVER THE PHONE

As I mentioned in chapter 9, I dislike pitching in person. I much prefer to sell over the phone without any video. Just my voice and the visual pitch deck. For me, this reduces distraction.

Some people may disagree with me and feel that face-to-face selling, or at least using video for sales presentations, is the only way to go. They like to be able to read nonverbal cues.

My advice, as it will be in every part of this section, is to do what feels right to you. We are our best and most authentic selves when we are in an environment that is comfortable for us. It's that simple.

Update: I originally wrote this section prior to the coronavirus pandemic of 2020. Many people who had not previously used web video conferencing have since been forced to communicate with family and friends via Zoom calls. My son even had workouts with his soccer team via Zoom. Crazy. As such, it's more acceptable than ever before to skip the car or plane ride but a bit less acceptable to turn off your video.

FUNNY VERSUS SERIOUS

Earlier in the book, we discussed using humor and cursing in your sales process, and I mentioned that you should only try to use humor or colorful language if you feel comfortable with those tools and they're appropriate for your situation.

If you do use dirty jokes, know that you can adjust your approach in each situation. I happen to use quite a bit of humor, and although I don't go out of my way to curse, I do tend toward the colorful. That said, sometimes I'm on calls where I have to restrain myself or use a more professional, corporate tone because it's clear the prospect will not respond well to my default approach.

Do what suits your style, but tailor it to the situation at hand.

FAST VERSUS SLOW

Rhythm in sales is important. In the chapter on presenting, I talked about setting a good pace and keeping the meeting moving toward its conclusion. I coached you to not let prospects grab the microphone and take over the meeting. All that said, what's fast for one may be slow to another.

Find a pace that suits your style but have the flexibility to slow down or speed up as the situation dictates. If you're on a call with a prospect who is well versed in the services you're discussing and has a fast pace, match it. If you sense a part of the presentation is not resonating, move on. If you're speaking with a newbie who's a bit more methodical, match them, but do so in your own voice and style.

These are just a few examples. The point is to adopt a style that feels authentic and comfortable for you, with an eye toward your prospect's style and pace.

The same coaching applies to any examples I've provided that include detailed scripts or email templates. You don't have to copy my closing scripts or emails verbatim. As long as you include the key elements, you can and should "make it your own."

Don't regurgitate what I've taught you like a robot. Have engaging conversations like a human. The human that *you* are, not the one I am.

CUSTOMIZING THE CLONE FOR COMMON CIRCUMSTANCES

As with your communication style, you can and should adjust the actual steps, stages, processes, and templates. Every agency is different, and you may need to rearrange or cut out some of the processes and templates I've presented. Here are a few examples.

CUSTOMIZING FOR YOUR TARGET AUDIENCE

If you sell to larger, relatively sophisticated companies, you may need a deep sales engineering process. If you sell to small, local yoga studios, a quicker, less in-depth approach (or no sales engineering at all) may be more appropriate.

As you create your own system based on the lessons in this book, ask yourself whether each step is necessary, unnecessary, or in need of modification based on the type of customer you're targeting.

Don't be afraid to test. Try your process with and without a particular element and see how it works for you. Start with as much of my system as seems appropriate and then refine it as you go.

CUSTOMIZING FOR YOUR AGENCY AND SERVICE TYPE

If you've decided to be a boutique, high-touch agency selling relatively expensive services to sophisticated clients, you probably need all the steps of the process I've outlined. If, however, you are a large agency selling inexpensive, cookie-cutter services to smaller clients, you may be able to greatly reduce the effort you put into developing and delivering custom strategies and presentations. You might go right from discovery into a pitch of one of your fixed-fee programs on the diagnosis call. If that works for your situation, go for it.

CUSTOMIZING FOR YOUR GOALS AND RESOURCES (AGENCY SIZE, FINANCIAL LIMITATIONS, ETC.)

If you're a freelancer with a limited budget and you want only one or two new clients a month, you probably don't need (and can't afford) to take a true team selling approach. Although that does not mean you can't hire an administrative assistant or outsource some parts of your marketing, you may do the diagnosis call, the sales engineering, and presentation of services all by yourself. And if that suits your situation, skills, and resources, great, do that.

However, if you're looking to grow your annual revenue to $10,000,000 and bring on ten new clients a month, you probably can't do that using only bits and pieces of the system and with one person on your sales and marketing team. You need to invest a good amount of money into building a sophisticated system with all the necessary marketing effort, software tools, and people to make it successful.

You're almost done! Don't skip the conclusion. I tie everything together and deliver the most important message in the entire book.

KEY TAKEAWAYS FROM CHAPTER 12

- Don't copy like a robot. Bring your personality to the party.

- Be authentic and choose an approach that suits your style with a nod to the prospect's personality.

- Skip and adjust steps and otherwise customize my system to your specific circumstances.

- Start with the parts of the system you feel are a good fit and will be most impactful. Don't be afraid to test and refine your system over time.

CONCLUSION

This book started with the following quote from Tony Robbins:

"If you want to be successful, find someone who has achieved the results you want and copy what they do and you'll achieve the same results."

When I started my career in internet marketing, everything was new, both to me and to business owners and marketers who wanted to take advantage of this weird thing called the World Wide Web.

There was no map of this strange land. No direct or obvious path to success. As each new marketing technology and innovation emerged (the web itself, websites for businesses, search engines, online advertising, social media, etc.), we had to scramble to learn how it worked and how it fit into the rapidly evolving marketing ecosystem.

It was not uncommon for people to try to apply strategies that worked well in the age of TV advertising to the internet. Some of those old approaches worked. Many felt like trying to jam a square peg into a round hole. Old tactics did not always apply to the new world of marketing, and because everything was so new, there was nobody to copy.

As the years passed, we learned from each other. We wrote and read books about internet marketing. We blogged about our case studies and success stories. We hosted and attended webinars. Tactical tips from a new crop of marketing gurus appeared in our email inboxes. We got better through trial and error, study, and sharing. We created and continue to create maps of the territory.

If you're starting in internet marketing now, there are plenty of successful people you can copy. Want to know how to run a successful Instagram influencer campaign? Interested in the fundamentals of SEO? For just about any digital marketing tactic more than six months old, you can be sure there is a book, a video course, or any number of educational resources dedicated to it.

When I made the transition from digital marketing practitioner to digital marketing salesperson, there was no digital-marketing-specific sales book for me to learn from. Instead, I read general sales books. I read articles and blogs about tried-and-true sales techniques from the past. I attempted to apply the old ways to the new digital services. As with marketing itself, some older sales tactics worked and some not so much. I walked through the fires of trial and error. I took notes along the way. Those notes became this book.

Although I have not done extensive research to confirm this, at the time of writing, I believe this is the first book laser-targeted on providing a detailed blueprint you can copy to sell more digital marketing services. Like those in the marketing world who came before me and left their notes, I want to share what I've learned on the sales trail. I hope the ideas in this book make your journey to sales success a bit more direct, quick, and easy.

To conclude, I'd like to provide a summary of the trail markers I've laid out and then give you what I believe is the most impactful advice in this book.

In part one, I discussed the importance of having a proven system—not only to enable efficiency and scalability but also to allow you to take a team selling approach instead of hiring expensive sales unicorns.

Next, we talked about the foundational work you can do to position your agency to win by identifying your ideal clients, creating Winnable Games, and offering unique value. Also, we sketched out the architecture of a successful sales system and the associated processes, steps, stages, tools, and templates.

In part two of the book, I covered the details of the system and provided an exact blueprint you can copy to build and run your own successful sales system. Here is a list of the core lessons from part two.

CHAPTER 4

Attract the leads you need by diagnosing your deficiencies and applying the three wheels of marketing with appropriate strategy, skill, and resources.

CHAPTER 5

Speed sells. Respond to leads as quickly as possible to maximize your chance of winning deals.

CHAPTER 6

Shift from order taker to strategic sales doctor by using the diagnosis call process and template.

CHAPTER 7

Use sales engineering and team selling to win more deals and create proposals that represent Winnable Games and improve client retention.

CHAPTER 8

Use a proven approach to presentation structure and slide design to tell stories that sell.

CHAPTER 9

Practice and refine eight core sales skills to ensure you deliver your presentations like an ace.

CHAPTER 10

Use authenticity, intentionality, and proven techniques to turn closing into a simple, direct invitation for your prospects to get the results you showed you can achieve.

CHAPTER 11

Be sure to set up tracking to monitor and manage your sales machine. Use tools, templates, and automation to maximize your efficiency and effectiveness.

CHAPTER 12

Customize the system to suit your situation and style. Start with the parts that appear to have the best chance of making an impact and then test and refine over time.

This book contains a tremendous amount of practical information. There are tons of actionable recommendations you can start to implement today. Before you do anything else, make sure you've done at least some of the foundational positioning work so you're not a generic brown box. If you do nothing else but improve your positioning, you'll attract more leads and win more deals.

Next, go back and scan the chapters to find one or two things you believe will have the most immediate impact. Typically, the approaches I've taught you in regard to the diagnosis process and to creating and delivering presentations make the biggest difference.

I'd like to leave you with one last recommendation—the most important one in this book.

THE BOTTOM LINE: BE WORTH DOING BUSINESS WITH

"A satisfied customer is the best business strategy of all."

—MICHAEL LEBOEUF

When a hailstorm rolls through a town and damages hundreds of homes, roofers from across the country descend like locusts. Homeowners have insurance checks in hand and are eager to hire someone to replace their roofs. The problem is that many roofers are shady or outright scam artists.

In 2012, my agency business partners and I started a side business to generate leads for storm-damage roofing contractors. The idea was to do background checks and training to certify roofers so homeowners knew who the good guys were.

One of the resources we used to certify applicants was their company's Better Business Bureau rating. A representative from the BBB told me that storm-damage roofing contractors have the highest rate of complaints of any type of business in any industry. Period.

In 2018, I was running a diagnosis call for one of my digital agency clients whose ideal client profile required prospects to seem like good people to work with. At the end of the call, I said, "Well, after speaking with you guys for a while, I think we may be a good fit. You have an e-commerce site [which is this agency's specialty], you are struggling with exactly the sort of SEO challenges we specialize in, and you seem like you have good personalities."

As soon as I made the comment about their personalities, I got a big laugh (which was not my intention). One of the prospects on the call said to their coworker, while still laughing, "Did you hear that? The SEO guy said we seemed like good people." I responded with, "Well, I'm not the SEO guy; I'm the salesperson. And I'm not sure which one has a worse reputation."

The point of these two stories is that the digital marketing industry has a real reputation problem. In the eyes of many prospects, we're almost as bad as roofing contractors. And it's been getting worse over the last few years.

I spoke earlier in the book about how nearly 80 percent of the prospects I interact with in sales situations are coming from agencies with which they are not happy. Many people have been burned more than once and are fed up with the bullshit that gets peddled as digital marketing services and the lack of profitable results.

It's not always the agency's fault. There are plenty of clients who are to blame for their own business and marketing failures. That said, there are a few areas agencies can and should clean up. If you do, you'll stand out as one of the good guys.

We've touched on most of these issues along the way, but they bear repeating.

SELLING SERVICES TO PEOPLE THAT DON'T NEED THEM

Just because someone calls and asks for Facebook advertising services does not mean you should sell them those services. If you take the time to understand their business and marketing goals and you believe Facebook advertising is not a good strategic fit, don't sell it to them. Sell them what you think they need. If you don't offer the services that you think are right for them, I believe it's your obligation to be transparent and provide good advice, even if that means losing a deal. Good doctors don't prescribe the wrong pills just because the patient asked for them, and they will refer a patient to a specialist if they know the medical services they offer are not the right solution. If you sell services people don't really need, eventually it will come back to bite you and damage your reputation.

SELLING PARTIAL SERVICES OR COOKIE-CUTTER SERVICES THAT WON'T PRODUCE GOOD RESULTS

Selling a super-basic $199-a-month link-building service when you know the prospect has little understanding of what a comprehensive SEO program requires is bad business. Either sell a comprehensive solution or at least be transparent and educate the prospect on what your service can and can't do for them. More on this in the next section.

SELLING A SERVICE THAT REQUIRES OTHER, COMPLEMENTARY SERVICES FOR IT TO WORK AND NOT MENTIONING IT TO THE PROSPECT

If a prospect wants to launch Google and Facebook advertising, for example, and you know that their website is dated and not going to convert well, I believe it's your duty to explain why a comprehensive solution that addresses the advertising and the landing pages is necessary to achieve their goals. By doing this, you avoid having your team deliver on their part but fail to achieve the client's marketing goals because nobody addressed the other parts of the marketing funnel.

Another common example is using digital marketing to

generate leads for a client who can't effectively handle the leads. I'm not saying you have to provide sales training, too, but you should at least make sure the client is aware of the lead volume you're going to drive and the sales skills necessary to turn your hard work into profitable new clients. I can't tell you how many times agency owners have told me a client fired them because they said the leads the agency was generating were no good, when it was really the client's fault for not being able to handle the leads effectively.

Don't sell cookies without at least mentioning the milk.

NOT CONNECTING SERVICES TO THE BUSINESS RESULTS THE PROSPECT WANTS AND FOCUSING ONLY ON VANITY METRICS

You can't pay your phone bill with Instagram followers. First-page Google rankings for keywords that have little to no search volume are useless. If you sell a content marketing program that promises three blog posts a month, simply producing the blog posts is not enough. Vanity metrics (or interim metrics) may be important but only if they ultimately lead to more money for your clients. Skip over this issue and your client retention will tank.

NOT SETTING REALISTIC EXPECTATIONS FOR TIME AND RESULTS

This is simple. Don't promise things that are unrealistic. Just because a client says they need their website up in two weeks, their ROAS to be 10X, or their SEO to start paying off after two months does not mean you have to agree to that. Agree to what you can, but always err on the conservative side. Make under-promising and over-delivering your mantra.

BEING SHITTY AT WHAT YOU DO

If you're going to do anything in life, do it well. I'm not saying everyone has to be number one or world class at everything. But if you're going to go through the trouble of running an agency, you should have good customer service, study your craft, and be better than average. Don't offer a service you aren't good at just to close a deal.

Not only will addressing the issues listed above help your agency attract more referrals and close more deals, but it will also help you retain clients longer and improve the overall reputation of our industry. Most importantly, you'll enjoy your job more, sleep better, and run a more profitable agency.

In the words of Steve Martin, be so good they can't ignore you.

Everything is easier when you're worth doing business with.

Happy selling!

If you have questions or need more hands-on help, I'd love to hear from you. I offer online courses, coaching, speaking, workshops, and comprehensive consulting.

Email me: forrest@solvesales.com

Learn more: www.clonetheace.com and www.solvesales.com.

ACKNOWLEDGMENTS

Salespeople get a bad rap. I was fortunate to grow up with one of the best in the world, my dad. Thank you for all the inspiration and support along the way. Much of what I have accomplished in life, including writing this book, stems from your advice. You encouraged me to have the balls to quit when something was not working but to never give up when the finish line was near.

Mom, thank you for showing me what love looks like. You were always there with a kind word or an open ear. No matter what was going on in your life, your children always came first. For that I'm eternally grateful.

Brother, thank you for being my biggest fan even when I did not return the favor. You are true and good like few I've ever met, and your unwavering belief in me has helped me believe in myself.

To Audrianna for your contribution to many of the stories shared in this book and your genius insights into my own psyche. Your ability to shine a light in the dark corners has inspired my creativity and helped bring many of my crazy ideas to life.

To John for giving me my first job in the internet marketing industry when I had no experience. It was the start of a journey that led to this book. And to all my coworkers who took the time to teach me internet marketing when I had never even heard of SEO or pay per click.

To Arron Kahlow for providing a national platform for me to speak and grow that contributed to my sales opportunities and skills.

To Rick, Chris, Clayton, and Todd for being the best business partners one could wish for. It was in the crucible of Clixo that this book was born. When I started selling internet marketing, you were the products. It was your insane skills and dedication to excellence that gave me the confidence to close all those deals and develop the processes that are the foundation of this book.

To Mike and all the great people at www.goinflow.com for providing the platform and freedom to finish what I started. It was in the heat of the battle, in the trenches with you that the finishing touches for this book were fully baked.

To Jay Mays for finding the time you did not have during the coronavirus pandemic to methodically and thoughtfully provide the detailed feedback necessary for finishing this book with flare.

To my coaches and mentors Nancy and Russell for the

endless encouragement. You got me through the tough times and continue to support me. For your love and wisdom, I am eternally grateful.

To Brett for your friendship. We helped each other through the down times, and now look at us! We turned each other into perennial home-run hitters.

And finally, to all the sales prospects and clients who often drove me crazy by asking good (and stupid) questions, ghosting me, and providing tricky sales and marketing problems for me to solve. You were my true teachers and provided the lessons in this book.

All of you were the fire that forged this ace.

ABOUT THE AUTHOR

FORREST DOMBROW is a serial entrepreneur and a sales consultant with seventeen years of experience in the online marketing industry. He has worked with hundreds of small and medium-sized businesses and has sold millions of dollars in digital marketing services to some of the largest brands in the world.

Forrest was named one of the Online Marketing Institute's Top 40 Digital Strategists in Marketing and is a featured speaker at some of the industry's most prestigious conferences. He lives, works, and golfs in Denver, Colorado. To learn more about Forrest and his solutions, visit www. clonetheace.com and www.solvesales.com.

Made in the USA
Las Vegas, NV
17 September 2021